EARTH

to

GLORY

The Biblical Doctrine of the Human Body

Jonathan H. Rainbow

Table of Contents

Foreword.....page i

Chapter 1......page 1
And Man Became a Living Creature

Chapter 2......page 13
You Will Surely Die

Chapter 3......page 26
Death at Work: Sickness

Chapter 4......page 44
The Outer Man Decays: Aging

Chapter 5......page 54
The Body of Jesus

Chapter 6......page 66
The Body to Come

Chapter 7......page 82
The Perversion of the Appetites

Chapter 8......page 101
Glorify God in Your Body

Chapter 9......page 116
How to Glorify God in Your Body

Afterword......page 138

Foreword

As a man grows older, he becomes more aware of and thinks more systematically about his body.

His own body weakens. As I write this, I'm 52. I'm a healthy and vigorous 52. I exercise regularly and hard, and I still weigh what I weighed when I was 20. But signs of aging and weakening do appear. Little things go wrong; broken parts heal more slowly; sleep is not as sound. When I was 20, my body was my slave; it did what I commanded and came back for more. Now, my body is my advisor; when it cautions I usually obey. I can envision a time coming when my body will be a tyrant. I think about this a lot.

Around him, a man's family and friends change and age. My friends look middle aged! My children, now 28, 26, and 24, look like adults. My two grandchildren have entered the world with their tiny, rubbery, delectable bodies and I reflect that my own children were once like that. I was once like that! On the other end, my own parents, now in their mid-seventies, are approaching death. My mother is in an advanced stage of Alzheimer's disease, and my father, still healthy for a 76 year old, is weakening. And I am only 24 years behind.

A man becomes more aware that human life is bodily life. The body is not an appendage, a stage prop, or a background fact. It is central to who we are and to how we live. Its needs – food, drink, rest, comfort – are at the center of civilization. Its lusts are at the center of many of our problems and crimes. Its repair and maintenance are a looming social and financial catastrophe as medical research gives us more, and more expensive, fixes. Our diversions and pleasures are things of the body – sports, music, recreation – and success and power are linked in some mysterious but undeniable way to physical beauty. A man becomes more sensitive to such things as he grows older.

This book is, therefore, to some extent the product of my own ruminations and evolving awareness of the body – a work of self reflection. But it is also the response of a theologian to the vagueness and sloppiness of much Christian thinking today. I've spent my adult life in the pastorate and then in the teaching profession, and I've found that there is very little systematic biblical instruction in the Christian community on important topics dealing with the body. It's almost as if we've abdicated this area of truth to the scientists, the doctors, the psychologists, and the religious TV hucksters. In particular, there is a huge empty spot in our theology where the doctrine of the resurrection of the body should be. Often, when Christians do talk about the body, it is in "platonic" rather than in biblical terms. This book will address the pernicious influence of "platonism" on Christians' thinking about their bodies.

The Christian faith, proceeding from the Bible, has much to say about the human body, its origin, its nature, its death and its destination. It has much to say to Christians about their bodily hope for the future and their life of obedience to Christ now, in the body.

Jonathan Rainbow
Visalia, California
October, 2003

CHAPTER 1

And Man Became a
Living Creature

The human body is a piece of God's creation, and its story begins, with all creation, in Genesis.

As we begin to read this story from our vantage point as modern, western evangelical Christians, we find that we are flanked by two competing doctrines of the human body, and that our investigation of Genesis must be, in part, an effort to steer between them.

These competing doctrines are *materialism* and *platonism*.

Materialism and platonism at the funeral home

Soft organ music plays in the background. Light from muted pastel fixtures falls on the scene: banks of flowers, a shiny coffin, open at the middle like a Dutch door, and a dead body face up within it. People file by to look once more at the person they knew alive. Outside, they break into small clusters and talk. In one, a man says:

"Well, John's gone. We'll miss him."

"Too bad. He was so young. He had more to offer."

In another small group, a relative of the dead man is saying:

"I don't like viewings. That's not John anymore, and it's a shame to show him that way. He's in a better place now." And others are nodding yes.

Two philosophies are being expressed here, as the living try to get their minds around death and make something of the brute fact of John's dead body. The first group is the John's Gone Group. For them, John is in the coffin and John is gone. John's body really was John, and John is dead, and as John's body decays into nothingness, John will decay into nothingness. The second group is the That's Not John Group (or perhaps, the Better Place Group). For them, the body in the coffin is the disposable shell of the "real" John, who continues to live in some nonmaterial afterlife.

These are the two dominant non-biblical doctrines of the human body – materialism and platonism – and since we will engage with these doctrines at every point in this study, it will be good to identify them clearly here.

Materialism: you're only matter

Materialism is the view that everything, including life, including human life, is matter. Everything is matter plus energy – atoms, gravity, radiation, electromagnetism, and whatever other arcane particles or forces have been discovered or posited by physicists. There is no "spirit," no supernatural, no "life" that lies outside matter plus energy, no "soul." No gods, no angels, no devil, no God. In human

2

life, love, hate, memory, aspiration, longing, speculation, faith, and joy are all matter plus energy. The *Mona Lisa*, Mozart's *Piano Concerto in D Minor*, and *The Brothers Karamazov* are all products of atoms plus energy.

Materialism is not a modern invention. Some of the Greeks suggested it, and one could argue, from a Christian perspective, that the life of the typical unbeliever is a kind of default materialism ("The fool has said in his heart, 'There is no God'"). But materialism as a self conscious way of interpreting the world has come into its own in the last century and a half in the company of secularized science and the doctrine of evolution. In his popular book *Cosmos*, Carl Sagan said, "The cosmos is all that is, all that ever was, and all that ever will be."[1] Surely Sagan was aware that this statement echoes the self definition of the biblical God, "who was, and who is, and who is to come," and surely he was asserting that in modern, enlightened thinking the universe itself has replaced God as the eternal verity.

If the cosmos is all that is and if the cosmos is matter, then man is also matter. In the gorgeous National Geographic book about the human body, *The Incredible Machine*, life is described as follows: "The stuff of stars has come alive. Inanimate chemicals have turned to living things that swallow, breathe, bud, blossom, think, dream."[2] How? Through the mystery of evolution, the transformation of "chemical to creature" in the "primordial sea."[2]

Evolutionists sometimes wax poetic about this mystery ("These evolutionary origins do not diminish us; they exalt us"[2]), but the plain fact remains, despite hymns to the contrary, that evolutionists are materialists and that for them man is matter. "With our bodies – biological galaxies of stellar dust – we are not only the center of the universe, we are more. We are the universe."[2] We are, that is to say, molecules. Molecules marvelously arranged, but molecules nevertheless. Our feelings are, ultimately, reducible to matter. Our thoughts are matter. When we die, we are gone. Our individual existences are no more than a temporary conglomerating of the "stuff of stars" on its way back to stardust.

Brutally and plainly put, without the garnish: we are simply our bodies.

Materialism is no longer, as it was at an earlier time in history, only for scholars and philosophers. It is popular culture. It is what many people believe about themselves and about their bodies.

If, that is, they are not platonists.

Platonism: matter doesn't matter

The term "platonism" comes from the name of the famous Greek philosopher, Plato. It's fair to say that Plato was a platonist, but the term "platonism," as I'll use it in this book, is not intended as a precise definition of Plato's thought. Instead, it is a general term, a convenient label for the doctrine that stands at the opposite end of the philosophical spectrum from materialism.

In platonism, matter exists, but it is not nearly as important as the unseen world of the spirit. Indeed, matter stands opposed to spirit. Beyond the material world perceived by the senses are God, spirit, and the soul. The material world is in a constant flux which tends toward disorder and degeneration, while the spiritual world is firm and pure. Man is a combination of matter and soul; he is an immortal soul inhabiting a mortal, dying, deteriorating body. The combination of body and soul is full of tension: the soul pulls upward, toward God, beauty, and good, while the body pulls downward, toward food, comfort, sex, and physical gratification. Human life, in platonism, is a struggle of the two temporarily conjoined components of man, body and soul. A good man is simply a man whose soul is winning, while a bad man is a man controlled by his physical appetites. At death, the soul is freed from the prison-house of the body to migrate either to heaven or, as for reincarnationists, to some other body.

The platonic doctrine of man had an enormous influence on early Christian theology; several important Christian theologians of the first three or four centuries of the church's history incorporated features of platonism into their writings. It's not difficult to understand the temptation to do this. Platonism had certain superficial resemblances to the Christian gospel: it was monotheistic, it proclaimed an unseen, spiritual world, and it exhorted humans to virtue and self denial. Its emphasis on the evil of the human body even sounded – although it was in fact not – similar to the biblical condemnation of the "flesh." So, through these early theologians, the concepts and the language of platonism, especially in regard to the nature of man, made their way into Christian theology. We will see, again and again, how this concept shows up in Christian thinking about man, salvation, and ethics.

The materialist says: *This body is me, all of me, and when I die I am no more.*

The platonist says: *This body is not me, it's only a shell, and when I die I'll be free of it.*

Seemingly diametrically opposed conceptions, and yet they have one thing in common. In both, there is no

5

future for the body, no eternity, no redemption. For both, the death of the body is final. And in both, death is accepted, whether as the inevitable natural end of a fleeting conglomeration of atoms or as the liberation of an imprisoned soul.

The biblical doctrine of the body does not accept death, nor does it accept the death of the human body as the end. The roots of the biblical doctrine are in creation, and in Genesis.

Man is like God

The creation account of Genesis 1 and 2 encompasses the creation of the entire universe, from the galaxies to the bugs, but it centers on what is clearly God's most remarkable work: his creation of man. The churning pace of Genesis 1 suddenly slows as God consults with himself in the creation of humanity: "Let us make man in our image, according to our likeness . . . and God created man in his own image, in the image of God he created him; male and female he created them" (Genesis 1:26-27, NASB). Alone of all the creatures, man is the "image of God," and whatever this means in detail, it certainly must mean in general that man reflects God's own nature in some unique way. So the emphasis of Genesis 1 is on the likeness of man to God.

Man is like the other creatures

In Genesis 2, however, the emphasis shifts. It is the same Creator and the same creature, but the camera is, as it were, positioned differently, because the theological point is different. In Genesis 2, it is not the likeness of man to God that is established, but the likeness of man to the other animate creatures. The details of the account of man's formation in Genesis make this clear. "Then the Lord God formed man of the dust from the ground, and breathed into his nostrils the breath of life; and man became a living creature" (Genesis 2:7).

Man's creation takes place in two stages. First, there is the "formation" of man from the dust of the ground. The Hebrew verb "to form," used in this verse, means to shape, mold, or fashion, as when an artist or potter works. The Lord's raw material was the "dust of the ground," which was actually clay, wet ground, since (v. 6) a fine mist had watered the earth. God made the first human out of clay, and when the Bible depicts the divine-human relationship as one between a potter and clay, it is not being metaphorical (Isaiah 29:16; Jeremiah 18:1-6; Romans 9:20-23). We are, in the most literal sense, clay, earth. The first human got his personal name from what he really was: *adam* ("earth, ground" in Hebrew). This same word, *adam*, is also the Old Testament's word for "humanity."

The Genesis account also tells us that the vegetable creation (2:9) and the animal and bird creation (2:19) were made from the earth. So in this respect man is exactly like plants and animals. If we are different from plants and animals (and we are), it is not because we were formed from different stuff.

The second stage of man's creation is "animation." After his formation from clay he is still an inert, lifeless corpse. Then God breathed into man's nostrils the "breath of life" and he became a "living creature."

What is a "living creature"?

The King James Bible has: "and man became a living soul." I have translated: "and man became a living creature." Something very important is at issue here, not merely as a question of translation but as a question of how we think about ourselves.

The worthy translators of 1611 may not have intended it this way, but the fact is that their phrase "living soul" has become a pillar for platonic thinking among Christians. All one has to do to see this illustrated is to put the King James version of Genesis 2:7 before a group of Christians today and ask them what it means. The reply will be: "It means that God first created Adam's body, and then created his soul." It is seen as one of the key prooftexts that humans, unlike other creatures, have souls. It is seen as a statement that distinguishes, separates, man from the animals.

It is true, linguistically, that the English word "soul" can mean "life", and is so used many other places in the KJV. Perhaps the translators of 1611 intended it this way, and meant to say, "and man became a living life," that is, he came to life. If so, they were fairly close to the true meaning of the statement. The problem is that the word "soul" also refers, in English, to the nonmaterial part of man's being, the part that separates from the body at death. It is a loaded word. And even if they intended "living life," we are justified in wondering why they did not use the same translation for the same Hebrew phrase as it occurs several other times in Genesis 1-2.

For Genesis 2:7 is not the only place in the creation account where we read this Hebrew phrase, *nefesh hayah*.

"Let the waters teem with swarms of *nefesh hayah* . . . and God created the great sea monsters, and every *nefesh hayah* that moves, with which the waters swarmed after their kind . . . And God said, Let the earth bring forth *nefesh hayah* after their kind; cattle and creeping things and beasts of the earth after their kind . . . to every beast of the earth and to every bird of the sky and to everything that moves on the earth in which is a *nefesh hayah*, I have given every green plant for food" (Genesis 1:20, 21, 24, 30). Even before the creation of man, the earth is full of *nefesh hayah*, living lives, living souls, living creatures – or whatever one chooses to call them. Fish are *nefesh hayah*; birds are *nefesh hayah*; land animals and creeping things are *nefesh hayah*. And, finally, man is *nefesh hayah*: "And the Lord breathed into his nostrils the breath of life, and man became *nefesh hayah*."

The real issue is not what the translation of this phrase is, but whether the same translation is used consistently throughout the Genesis creation account. It should be. The point is clearly that man is the same as the other creatures. Any translation – like the KJV – which uses one translation for the animals and another for man, misses and obscures the point. The KJV suggests to the average person that man has a "soul" and animals don't, which is true, but which is not the point of the passage. The "breath of life" is not the human soul, but life itself, animation, which man shares with all living, moving creatures. So I prefer to translate all the occurrences of this phrase, in Genesis 1 and 2, "living creatures."

As I consult six well known English translations, I find that not a single one captures this point of correspondence between man and the other living creatures of the earth. All of them follow the KJV in using one phrase for animals and another for man. Even Luther, in his German translation, does the same. Why? Are we afraid to be reminded that we are creatures like other creatures, made from clay, animated by God? Does the radical dependence on God that this implies offend us? But there is no need to fight the battle for man's uniqueness on the field of Genesis 2:7, for Genesis 1:28 has already clearly pronounced us to be the "image of God."

Man is the image of God. Man is also a living creature, like other living creatures which move on the earth.

Let's draw some implications from this, implications which will be the underpinnings of much that follows in this book.

Man is more than matter

Genesis discredits materialism as a view of man. A human being is more than mere matter. He is in some sense like God rather than like the rest of creation. Man is rational, spiritual, ethical, and shares these characteristics only with the angels among God's creatures. And man, though he has a beginning like other creatures, does not have an end. And – although this is not the meaning of Genesis 2:7 – man is a soul as well as a body.

Man is a physical-spiritual whole

Genesis also discredits platonism as a view of man. A human being is an integrated whole. He is a complex, double-sided creature who possesses a God-likeness as well

10

as an animal-likeness, and his nature is capable of being separated into physical and spiritual components (which is what happens at physical death), which the Bible denotes as "body" and "soul" ("Do not be afraid of those who can kill the body but not the soul" - Matthew 10:28). But in the biblical doctrine of man, the body and soul belong together; they are not pitted against each other as a lower and higher nature as they are in platonism. In platonism, body and soul are unnaturally and uncomfortably stapled together. In the Bible, body and soul are integrated as the warp and woof of a cloth, or as the stereo tracks of a music recording, distinguishable but not independent. In platonism, physical death is the deliverance of the soul from the entanglement of the body. In the Bible, physical death is the tearing apart of an organism.

The body is the person, your body is you

Genesis establishes that the body of a person is that person. Your body is you. It is not all you are, but it is genuinely you. It is not a shell, or a container. It is man, *adam*. God intends human life to be bodily life, and that's why, in spite of the creeping platonism which causes people to say "that's not really John" at funerals, we are still saddened by death. It's why even the people who talk platonically don't just toss John's body into the dumpster, but treat it with dignity and respect. It's why there will be a resurrection of the dead.

The body is good

Genesis also establishes that the body is good. When

God the Creator had surveyed all that he had made, he concluded, "And behold, it was very good" (Genesis 1:31). This is a point which separates biblical truth radically from platonism. In platonism, matter in general and the body in particular are bad; the body pulls downward; the body tends to corrupt whatever the soul aspires to by its base and repulsive appetites. But in the Bible, man's body is good. It is true that the body has been profoundly affected by sin. But so have the human thinking, feeling, and willing. In the Bible it is not the body that is evil, but man in his wholeness who has become evil through rebellion against his Creator and who has suffered in all his existence the consequences of his own depravity. The body is sinful, not because it is a body but because it is you, and you are sinful.

The body is man, and the body is good. But we must come back to the corpse in the coffin. Something has gone wrong.

[1] Sagan, Carl, *Cosmos*, Ballantine Books, 1985
[2] National Geographic Society, *The Incredible Machine*, 1986

CHAPTER 2

You Will Surely Die

No matter how hard we try, we can't get used to death.

We've tried. The philosophers and the psychologists and the scientists have done their best to domesticate death, to provide humans, who all face certain death, with some other way of thinking and feeling about death than that which instinctively comes to them: fear, revulsion, and anger. The fox in Aesop's fable couldn't obtain the grapes so he persuaded himself that they must not be good after all, illustrating the human tendency to reinterpret reality. With death, it's the opposite. Death is something we don't want but must have, and our reinterpretation is that, since we can't avoid it, it must not be so bad after all. But we know, as the fox did, that this is a trick we are playing on ourselves.

We have to think some way about death, and what we think about death is largely a function of what we think about the body.

The materialist: one time around

The materialist, who thinks that man is only his body, sees death as a natural, normal, inevitable event in the cycle of life. We are born, we grow, we flourish, we reproduce, and we die. That's the way it is, and we only subject ourselves to needless anguish if we struggle against this brute reality. Logically, of course, we want to maintain our existence as long and as happily as possible; we want to use modern medicine to the best possible advantage; we cultivate youthfulness and beauty, even to the point of liposuction and plastic surgery. But in the end, inexorably, the conglomeration of molecules will dissolve and we will be no more. That's nature. And in the modern intellectual climate, where "science" is the true religion and "nature" is all there is, what's natural is also good. This is the materialistic domestication of death.

The platonist: dead at last!

If the materialist domesticates death by reducing it to nature, the platonist does so by interpreting it as a liberation. This, too, rests on a basic view of the body: man is a body fastened to a soul, and death merely undoes this fastening. The soul is freed from the ball and chain of bodily existence. Plato's mentor, Socrates, explained to his weeping disciples before his state-compelled suicide, "True philosophers make dying their profession, and . . . to them of all men death is the least alarming." Why do philosophers look so kindly on death? Because "purification . . . consists in separating the soul as much as possible from the body."[3] Contrast Socrates' easy embracing of death with the terror of death

14

experienced by Jesus on the night before his crucifixion, his honest prayer to the Father to be spared the torture of crucifixion, his harsh rebuke of the friends who were too sleepy to share his anguish, his sweating, his churning emotions.

It is true that the apostle Paul says that "to die is gain" (Philippians 1:21), but this is not at all the same as the platonic longing for the liberation of the soul. It will be one of our tasks in this study to clarify the difference between the two conceptions.

In materialism, death is natural. In platonism, death is good. In the Bible, and for the Christian, death is a curse and an enemy.

The death threat was carried out the same day

The biblical doctrine of death, like the doctrine of the human body, is grounded in the early chapters of Genesis. We hear about it first as a mere threat: "For in the day that you eat from it [the tree of the knowledge of good and evil] you will surely die" (Genesis 2:17). The world into which this threat came was a world without death but over which the sword of the death threat hung, suspended on the thin fiber of man's continuing submission to his Creator as absolute Lord. Only one tree in the garden was forbidden. But Adam was unwilling to submit, even in this symbolic way, to the sovereignty of God; the fiber snapped; the sword of death descended just as God had warned that it would.

And it is worth noting that the original sin was a sin of the whole human: "When the woman saw that the tree was good for food, and that it was a delight to the eyes, and that the tree was desirable to make one wise, she took from

15

its fruit . . ." (Genesis 3:6). Hunger, visual pleasure, and prideful curiosity were all involved. The fall did not consist of a base body dragging down a noble soul, but of two whole persons – body and soul – rebelling against God and placing their mental and physical desires above the will of God.

God had told them that when they ate of the forbidden tree, they would die. It was a clear threat of immediate, summary punishment by death. It is not enough to say that eventually they died, although the grim litany, "and he died," which quickly begins in Genesis 5, certainly emphasizes that they did. But something happened to them immediately, on the very day of their crime, that constitutes death.

What happened, after a short trial, was that Adam and Eve were expelled from the garden of Eden. "So he drove the man out" (3:24). This expulsion from Eden was not a mere inconvenience, or even the first refugee experience. It was a spiritual catastrophe. It was the death of Adam, of Eve, and of the human race.

The garden was a fabric, a system, a network of relationships. It was, to begin with the most important thing, the place of man's fellowship with God, symbolized by the "tree of life." When God expelled Adam and Eve from the garden, he placed an angel with a flaming sword at the entry of the garden to "guard the way to the tree of life" (3:24). The way of access to God's manifest presence, friendship, and companionship, with all that such a relationship implied – namely, life – was thus barred.

The fabric of man's created life included not only his relationship with God the Creator but also his relationship with his fellow humans and the rest of the creation, over which God had given him dominion. The garden was a place of order, designed by God for man's good, where man was to live in a relationship of blessedness and peace with the other things that God had made for his own glory and for man's good. The vegetation would sustain man's life; the animals would serve him and keep him company. And man, male and female, would marry and multiply, and would – it seems to me – gradually extend the sphere of order and dominion from the garden to the whole face of the earth. In other words, the earth would become one large garden, in the same sense that Eden was a garden. Husbands would love wives, and wives husbands, and children parents; the human family would grow in number without any corresponding loss of order, happiness, or intimacy; the creation would be ruled but not raped, the animals used but not abused; and, holding all else together, human beings would worship and love the Creator above all things and the tree in the middle of the garden would continue to be untouched.

The garden was the beginning, the prototype, the seedbed of this future. When God drove man from the garden, it all vanished. God was no longer friend, but foe and prosecutor. The earth was no longer an ally and servant, but an adversary to be fought with toil and sweat, and the animals would eventually, in a development that took some time, become man's meat (Genesis 9:3). Fellow humans became objects of envy, contempt, and competition, as the murder of Abel by his brother Cain would shortly show.

Being driven by the wrath of God from the garden of Eden was death. Death in the Bible is the disintegration of man, imposed upon him by God in punishment for his

17

rebellion, the unraveling of man's existence in the complexity of his relationships – to God, to the world, to his fellow, and even to his own inner self. When the link with God snaps, everything else breaks apart. As Adam and Eve stood for the first time outside the boundaries of Eden, they were a dead man and a dead woman walking, alienated from their Creator, locked in a deadly struggle with the world around them, at war with one another, and headed for the dissolution of their own persons at that moment when they would give up the "breath of life" and when their bodies would return to the elements of the earth from which they had been formed.

Death is the opposite of creation. Death is un-creation. It is not a single, momentary event, but a process.

The stages of death

Systematic theologians, who explain the logical arrangement of biblical truth, sometimes speak of death in three stages: spiritual death, physical death, and eternal death. This is a helpful and fundamentally biblical arrangement.

As children of Adam, our human inheritance is spiritual death. We are spiritually stillborn; we begin our existence outside the garden, "dead in trespasses and sins" and "children of wrath" (Ephesians 2:1,3). Our minds are darkened, our wills are enslaved, our hearts are stone cold dead toward our Creator. But even in spiritual death, something remains of the original life: we still live on God's earth, we still breathe God's air, and we still enjoy the integrity of our persons in that body and soul are joined.

Much of this is sharply ended by physical death, in which the integrity of body and soul is dissolved and normal creaturely life on earth is cut off. The book of Revelation calls physical death the "first death" (Revelation 20:6).

Beyond physical death there lies only the radical and eternal disintegration of the "second death," eternal punishment, the lake of fire. The grim biblical images of hell – lake of fire, outer darkness, eternal destruction – certainly mean, whatever else they mean, the eternal and absolute exclusion of humans from the friendly presence of God, and the unending un-creation of the whole person.

Still, there remains something unique and decisive about physical death, that which we ordinarily call "death." Physical death is each man's Rubicon, his point of no return. "It is appointed to men to die once, and after this comes judgment" (Hebrews 9:24). Before physical death, death is reversible through conversion. But there is no evangelism in Hades, and there will be no judgment day conversions. Then it will be too late. We have an instinctive and accurate feeling of finality about physical death. And physical death is the one clear manifestation of death which everyone must acknowledge; the humanist may deny the reality of spiritual death, and the materialist may scoff at the concept of a lake of fire, but both must bury their friends, and both will die.

In the boxing ring with death

How then should a Christian believer feel about death?

Not, as the materialist, that death is "natural." And not, as the platonist, that death is "good." Death is bad. Death is not normal. Death is an affront, an obscenity, and

19

an enemy.

We are in the ring against this enemy, and from this bout we cannot escape. So what is the Christian strategy?

See how the materialist boxes. He steps into the ring with death knowing that he's going to be knocked out. He doesn't know when, but he knows that it will happen. He has no thought of victory. His only purpose is to buy as much time as possible and to acquit himself well. It is a comfort to him that, after all, death gets everybody.

The platonist can only chuckle at the crude foolishness of the materialist. The platonist doesn't even bother to put on his gloves. After all, he is looking forward to getting knocked out, and realizes that the "enemy" is really doing him a big favor. When the bells sounds, he offers his chin to the enemy, Socrates-style.

But Christians are neither materialists nor platonists. We take our direction from the Bible, and our definitions from Genesis. How should we deal with death?

Call it by its name

One thing that we can immediately do in the Christian community is to clean up our language, which is currently filled with death euphemisms and pious jargon. Uncle John didn't die, he "passed away," or "passed on," or is "not with us anymore." We say these things to avoid saying the words "death," "dead," and "died." We don't gain anything by sanitizing this enemy.

Let death hurt (listen to Job and to Jesus)

Along the same lines, we need to stop saying at

Christian funerals that we're not really grieving for the dead person, who after all is in heaven with the Lord, but for ourselves and our loss. It is true, of course, that we feel loss. And it is true that the soul of a believer is in heaven with Jesus, in which fact we must rejoice. But it is not true that we are totally happy and content about what has happened to this dead person. Something terrible has happened. The integrity of the person has been shattered; the dead body before us in the coffin is proof. This human person, as God created him or her, has been broken. And we grieve not only for ourselves but for him. We need to be more honest. We need to allow ourselves to be offended by death.

The Old Testament has something valuable to teach us here, because its doctrine of death presumes the radical integrity of the human person in body and soul, and because the Old Testament saints had to deal with death during a preliminary stage of God's revelation during which the truths of the presence of the soul with God and the resurrection of the body in the future were more obscure. In general, death in the Old Testament is regarded as a separation from the presence of God as that presence is enjoyed in earthly life. "For there is no mention of you in death: in Sheol [the place of the death, the NT Hades] who will give you thanks?" (Psalm 6:5) "What profit is there in my blood, if I go down to the pit? Will the dust praise you? Will it declare your faithfulness?" (Psalm 30:9) Heman the Ezrahite describes "the slain who lie in the grave, whom you remember no more, and they are cut off from your hand," and he asks rhetorically, "Will you perform wonders for the dead? Will the departed spirits rise and praise you? Will your lovingkindness be declared in the grave, your faithfulness in Abaddon [destruction]?" (Psalm 88:5,10,11)

These, remember, are statements of Old Testament *believers*, not of pagan skeptics; they are the honest facing of death in ignorance of the truths of eternal life that we as New Testament believers take for granted. What is significant is how the Old Testament writers never try to dodge the seriousness of death, or lapse into euphemisms or various methods of escape. Death is to them a dreadful thing. The separation of the body and the spirit of man is not deliverance but destruction. They don't want to die; they want to live. On this background, those utterances of the Old Testament saints which rise above this, and which lay hold of a life with God which follows death, and even of the resurrection of the body, are all the more extraordinary. "You will not abandon my soul to Sheol, neither will you allow your holy one to undergo decay. You will make known to me the path of life; in you presence is fullness of joy; in your right hand there are pleasures *forever*" (Psalm 16:10-11). These resurrection words of David become the resurrection words of Christ. Asaph, bemoaning the injustice that characterizes human life in the present, concludes that justice will be done in eternity: "With your counsel you will guide me, and afterward receive me to glory" (Psalm 73:24). The hope of eternal life is not absent from the Old Testament, but it does arise out of a sober view of death as something to be avoided and feared. Death is an enemy.

As Job watched his own body disintegrate, he was able to say: "I know that my redeemer lives, and at the last he will take his stand on the earth. Even after my skin is destroyed, yet from my flesh I shall see God, whom I myself shall behold, and whom my eyes shall see, and not another" (Job 19:25-27). This was a magnificent moment in the history of the Spirit's revelation of truth. The horror of death, the conviction of the integrity of the person, and the hope of resurrection lie mingled together in Job's statement. In its fundamental assumptions about the body and about death it is a thoroughly Old Testament statement; in its hope for the future it is a proclamation of the gospel of the resurrection of the dead.

In the New Testament, it is clearly revealed that the souls of believers are with Christ immediately after death, and that the bodies of believers (and, indeed, of all humans) will be raised. The pervading emotion is joy and the pervading mood is victory. How could it be otherwise after Jesus comes out of his grave? Nevertheless – and this is often overlooked – there is no romanticizing of death in the New Testament. It is never handled flippantly, as if it were anything but a forbidding enemy. The Old Testament has Job, reaching out for resurrection in the midst of decay, but the New Testament has Jesus, weeping over death in the face of resurrection as he stands by Lazarus' tomb. Why did Jesus weep? Not at his own loss, since he knew he would have his friend back with him shortly. Nor, as has been suggested, at the sadness of bringing Lazarus back from heaven – this idea has a certain kind of logic, but the raising of dead people is always a happy event in the New Testament (see Acts 20:10-20). Only one explanation for Jesus' weeping seems plausible. He was simply struck in his emotions at the horror and sadness of death as he faced it in the person of Lazarus, and he gave death its due by weeping about it before he called Lazarus out of the grave.

The apostle Paul also cringed in the face of physical death. It is true that to him "to die is gain" (Philippians 1:21), but it is a gain, an improvement, over the bodily life that Paul experienced on earth, full of tribulation, suffering, and temptation. In comparison to this assaulted, compromised life, being with Christ in spirit will be gain. But this is not the same as saying that death is good, or desirable. "For indeed while we are in this tent we groan, being burdened [that is, the present life in the body is difficult], because we do not want to be unclothed [stripped of bodily existence, dead], but to be clothed, in order that what is mortal [the present body] may be swallowed up by life [the resurrection body]" (II Corinthians 5:4). Paul doesn't want no body; he wants a new body. He is a Christian, not a platonist, and an apostle of Christ, not of Socrates. His real longing is not death, but resurrection, and if to get to resurrection he must pass through death, then it will be gain. He would prefer death to the present life because it means the enjoyment of the Lord's presence – "we prefer rather to be absent from the body and to be at home with the Lord" (II Corinthians 5:8) – but he would most prefer a direct transition of the life of the present body to the life of the resurrection body, which will be the experience of Christians who are still alive at the coming of the Lord.

Jesus wept at Lazarus' grave. Paul did not want to be without his body. Death in the New Testament remains – in spite of the clear vision of eternal life and resurrection – a hostile, abnormal, horrible thing.

The New Testament deals with death, not by transmuting it into something good and acceptable, but by facing it as an enemy and crushing it on the field of battle. The life of Jesus Christ overwhelms death. And the attitude of the Christian believer toward death should therefore be defiance.

Get defiant

The Christian, thinking biblically, looks death in the eye, not submissively (as the materialist) or amicably (as the platonist), but defiantly. He joins the battle belligerently, even though death looms over him with powerful menace. And death indeed delivers the first blow. It's a roundhouse right, and the Christian goes down, dead. It looks like the end of the fight. But while death celebrates its apparent victory, the Christian's soul goes directly to heaven into the presence of Christ, which is "very much better" (Philippians 1:23) and "gain" (1:21). This blessing of immediate fellowship with Christ at death, which is called the "intermediate state," is God's first overcoming of the power of death, but it is not the final victory. For the dead Christian rises from the dead and delivers his own lethal counterpunch which destroys death and wins the victory. This is the resurrection of the body. Death is not only foiled, it is reversed and defeated. The body of man is redeemed; the essentiality of the body to man's personhood is maintained; the goodness of the body, as God created, is established forever.

Death is curse. Death is un-creation. Death is the great enemy that God defeats in the salvation of his people.

But we don't meet death only at funerals and graveyards. We live with bodily death throughout our lives in the form of sickness and aging, and it is to those related topics that we must turn next.

[3] Plato, *The Last Days of Socrates*, Penguin Books, 1982

CHAPTER 3

Death at Work: Sickness

A modern American would probably be appalled, in any pre-modern society, by the visibility of sickness. In ancient Egypt, or imperial Rome, or medieval Europe, virtually nothing was curable. People stayed chronically sick with illnesses that we can quickly banish with medicines. Half of children died before their first birthday. The human body was a free fire zone for infections and diseases.

Now we have subdued many of these ancient killers. We live longer, and more of our infants survive. Really sick people don't remain at home, or on the streets, mingling among us, so we don't see them as much. We have, it seems, gained ground against the illnesses of the body. But the gains are not as impressive as they seem. For what we have really done is to replace one team of killers with another – at least in the industrialized world. While we hold the microbes at bay, we ingest and inhale things that the bodies of medieval people did not have to deal with. And, while their bodies fell prey to diseases of malnutrition, ours are crumbling under the sheer weight of food that we hurl against them. It's really not as different as we think. Everybody's body dies of something.

Physical illness, whether in the 10th or the 21st century, is the far off trumpet blast of death. It is death already at work. Sickness is the disintegration of man's physical existence, the un-creation of the state of peace and well-being that God established when he formed the bodies of Adam and Eve. After the first humans had been expelled from the garden, the day certainly came – perhaps quickly – when one said to the other, "I don't feel well at all." Since then, sickness has been the lot and the curse of fallen humans.

That includes Christians. We need to understand what is happening when we get sick, and how to think and pray about it.

The lesson of the law of Moses: sickness is punishment and curse

The earliest relevant biblical teaching comes as part of the law of Moses. The Lord promised Israel that if they would obey his commandments, he would spare them from the diseases which he had sent upon the Egyptians, for "I, the Lord, am your healer" (Exodus 15:28). He promised under the same conditions (obedience and loyalty) to "remove sickness from your midst" (Exodus 23:35, also Deuteronomy 7:15). Conversely, the Lord solemnly warned that disobedience to his commands would result in his cursing them "with consumption and with fever and with inflammation and with fiery heat ... and with the boils of Egypt and with tumors and with the scab and with the itch, from which you cannot be healed ... extraordinary plagues

27

on you and your children, even severe and lasting plagues and miserable and chronic sicknesses" (Deuteronomy 28).

The physical health of the Israelites under the law depended on their obedience to his commands. The older theologians called this linkage of blessing and obedience the "covenant of works." The apostle Paul sees this principle summarized in Leviticus 18:5: "So you shall keep my statutes and my judgments, by which a man may live if he does them." (See Galatians 3:12 and Romans 10:5.) The fulcrum word of the law was IF. If they kept God's commands, they would be healthy; if not, they would be sick.

Of course, as Paul explains in Galatians and Romans, this IF of the law was a death knell, for nobody, not even God's own chosen and favored people Israel, could keep his commands. The law, Paul explains, was in fact given in God's larger purpose to reveal precisely this impossibility and so to prepare the way for the perfect obedience of Jesus Christ and justification by faith in him alone. But while the law of Moses was in force, teaching its lesson, it was a heavy burden. It dealt curse, and death, because nobody kept it. And it dealt sickness too.

Because of the IF of the law, Israelites were supposed to understand their sicknesses as punishment from God. Sickness was curse. It is likely that for the typical Israelite of the old covenant, sickness was the most direct and frequent reminder of God's displeasure with his sin. Certain generations of Israelites were spared the invasions and conquests that were also promised by God as punishment for sin. Only some were carried away into exile. But all got sick, and if their lives were at all typical of pre-modern people, they got sick often and severely. And if you were a sick Israelite, you were supposed to say, "I've sinned, and

28

God is punishing me as he warned in the law." That's what the law taught you to think.

This points back to the fact that sickness is, theologically considered, simply death already at work. What is true of death is then also true of death's trumpet and precursor, sickness: it is God's punishment and curse.

The living death of leprosy

The Lord of Israel singled out one disease in particular and assigned to it a legal and spiritual meaning which captures this association of sickness, curse, and death in a graphic way. This disease was leprosy. Leprosy is one of those fearful afflictions which has been tamed by modern medicine; it is to us, living in a post-penicillin civilization, merely a curiosity from the past. But it must have been to the people of the ancient world an especially appalling thing because of the slow pace of the death it dealt and the terrible visible disintegration it worked upon the human body. Perhaps for these reasons, the leper in Israel became by God's ordinance a living embodiment of perpetual, irreversible ceremonial uncleanness. "As for the leper who has the infection, his clothes shall be torn, and the hair of his head shall be uncovered, and he shall cover his mustache and cry, 'Unclean, unclean!' He shall remain unclean all the days which he has the infection; he is unclean. He shall live alone; his dwelling shall be outside the camp" (Leviticus 13:45-46).

Outside the camp. Awful words, if we understand that the camp was the place of God 's presence and fellowship with his covenant people, and that to be placed outside the camp was to be cut off not only from Israel but

29

from God. What happened to the leper was essentially what had happened to Adam and Eve when they sinned. They were driven from God. They died, even though they walked and breathed and slept and reproduced. So the leper under the law of Moses was ritually dead. His sickness was the early visitation of death. On the background of this conception of leprosy, the work of Jesus with lepers appears as much more than just "healing." His willingness to mingle with lepers was the signal of a new covenant, his power to cure them was the trumpet blast of a new kingdom, and the lepers who walked away whole were people raised, as it were, from the dead.

Sin and sickness in the Old Testament

Often in the Old Testament sickness is the immediate curse of God for specific sins. On one occasion Aaron and Miriam, the brother and sister of Moses, grumbled against Moses' leadership. The Lord called them all to the tabernacle, rebuked Aaron and Miriam, and "the anger of the Lord was aroused against them, and he departed. And when the cloud departed from above the tabernacle, suddenly Miriam became leprous, as white as snow" (Numbers 12:9-10). Miriam's leprosy coincides with separation from God's presence; her disease is the embodiment of a living death. The story has a happy ending when the Lord takes away Miriam's leprosy at Moses' intercession, but the connection of sickness and death is clear. Gehazi, the servant of the prophet Elisha, was not so fortunate: for his greedy pursuit of the riches of Naaman, God gave him the leprosy which had only a short time before been miraculously removed from Naaman (II Kings

30

5:27). And Uzziah was struck with leprosy after entering the temple (II Chronicles 26:16-20).

Jehoram, the wicked king of Judah, after a bloody and idolatrous reign, was struck by God with a hideous intestinal disease that caused his intestines to slowly come out, "and he died in severe pain" (II Chronicles 21:19). This illness had been predicted by the prophet Elijah, and was a specific punishment from God.

In a vivid instance of the principle that the sins of the fathers are visited upon the sons, the baby son of David, the issue of his adulterous affair with Bathsheba, was struck ill. The illness lasted seven days, and was clearly a punishment upon David for his sin. In this case sickness led quickly to death (II Samuel 12:13-18).

Job's sickness and the sovereignty of God

An exception to this linkage of sickness and sin is the illness of Job. Job knows that God is responsible for his pain, and at first resists the temptation – posed to him by his wife – to curse God. But as the pain continues, Job begins to raise blunt questions about the justice of God. Most people who see Job as a model of quiet, submissive suffering only read the first two chapters. Job accuses God of arbitrarily afflicting him, of taking unfair advantage of his sovereign power. Job's friends want to help him but can only offer the standard explanation, the one that would be familiar to them as Old Testament people, that Job must have committed some terrible sin and that God is punishing him. Job knows that this does not explain the facts: he is not sinless, but neither is anyone else, and he had not sinned in some spectacular way which would explain why God has singled him out for suffering.

Both Job and his friends are working out of the Old Testament premise that sickness is a punishment for sin. The friends are saying: you are sick, so you must have sinned. Job is saying: I haven't sinned extraordinarily, so it is unjust for God to punish me extraordinarily. Job's friends think that Job is unrighteous. Job thinks that God is unrighteous.

Only Elihu, the youngster, has it right. God is the sovereign creator. God can do whatever he wants. We don't measure God's righteousness by some external criterion; rather, we measure it by what God does. We worship him even in his hard inscrutability. Both Job's friends and Job are called eventually to repentance, and Job worships God. His illness is not a punishment for sin, but a test, a learning experience, and a demonstration of the sovereignty of God.

So the conception of sickness, and of suffering in general, that emerges from the story of Job transcends the doctrine of the law of Moses, that sickness is punishment for sin. What Job learned is more nearly what the New Testament believer must learn than what the people of God experienced under the law of Moses. And what Job came to hope in, when convinced that his disease would kill him, is exactly the hope of the New Testament: the resurrection of the body.

The sicknesses of the Messiah

Before leaving the Old Testament, we must look at the important fifty-third chapter of Isaiah, which foretells the suffering and death of Jesus Christ as the substitute for his people. "He was despised and rejected by men, a man of sorrows and acquainted with *sicknesses*" (53:3). Although this word is traditionally translated "griefs," it is the Hebrew word "sicknesses," the same word used in Deuteronomy 28:59 and 61, where sicknesses are threatened as the punishment of God for disobedience to the law. Again, in Isaiah 53:4, the same word: "Surely he has borne our *sicknesses* and carried our sorrows . . ." Do the translators, do Christians in general in our antibiotic civilization, have some prejudice against the image of a sick Jesus, a coughing Jesus, a Jesus afflicted with stomach flu or fever or headache?

Isaiah's astounding prophetic picture is of a Messiah loaded down with the whole lethal load of human cursedness, including sickness. As a result of this full participation in the lot of fallen humans, the Messiah appears to observers as an especially cursed and wretched man: "He was despised, and we did not esteem him . . . we esteemed him stricken, smitten by God and afflicted" (53:3-4). The Old Testament nexus of sickness, suffering, and death with God's punishment for sin is visible here. Because of the Messiah's human sufferings, men will look at him and conclude, along the lines of the law of Moses, that he is a particularly sinful man, odious to God. They will regard him much as Job's three friends regarded Job. And the prominence of the concept of "sickness" in Isaiah 53:3-4 indicates that physical sickness will be part of that which brings the observers to consider him "smitten by God."

We will have more to say about the body of Jesus in a later chapter. It is clear from Isaiah 53, at least, that Jesus shared the common human susceptibility to illness. But it is possible that the prophecy is picturing a Messiah with *more than his share* of sickness, a man who endures a heavy measure of pain and discomfort, not only at his final suffering and death but through the whole course of his life. The Messiah is no "superman," but a man so lowly, so humble, so weak and sick, that those who look upon him think he must be the greatest of sinners.

In a sense this is true. Jesus has become at the hand of God the greatest of sinners – but only because he bears on his person, on his human body and in his holy soul, the sins and sorrows and pains of so many sinners. "He was wounded for our transgressions . . . the Lord has laid on him the iniquity of us all" (53:5,6). He "had done no violence, nor was any deceit in his mouth. Yet it pleased the Lord to bruise him; he has put him to grief" (53:9,10). The sicknesses that Jesus experienced, whatever and how many they were, were the sicknesses of his people, the preliminary workings of the curse of death within our bodies, disintegration and decomposition and un-creation visited upon us for our sins. Yet they were laid on Jesus Christ our substitute. And we must confess with wonder that the bodily sufferings of Jesus for us did not just commence with the flogging he received at the hands of the official executioners, but with his very entry into our fallen human existence as a man with a body. Perhaps this is part of what the apostle Paul has in mind when he tells us that the divine Son of God "emptied himself, taking the form of a servant, and being founded in the likeness of men," (Philippians 2:7), where it is clearly the apostle's point that the humiliation of Christ did not consist simply of his death on the cross but of his whole existence as a man.

Isaiah's prophecy, therefore, as it touches on the topic of sickness, is grounded on the Old Testament doctrine of sickness as punishment, but proclaims the good news that the substitute takes that punishment in our place.

34

Should Christians get sick?

An important question arises here: does Jesus' bearing of our sicknesses mean that believers should no longer be sick? Many claim that this is the case, and proclaim to Christians that they have, on the basis of Isaiah 53, the right to deliverance from sickness. Anything less than full health, it is proclaimed, comes from a lack of faith or a failure to understand the resources that are in Christ. Believers are supposed to "claim" by faith what Christ has purchased by his death, and that includes health.

If the Old Testament believer was to say, "I am sick because I have sinned," then the Christian – according to the "faith claim" teaching – is to say, "I am sick because I don't have enough faith." This opens up a nasty Pandora's box of implications and twisted logic, for the fact is that Christians do get sick like other people. I was once told by a Christian friend, who held a faith-claim viewpoint, that I shouldn't have the cold that I had, that Christ had taken that away on the cross. Perhaps uncharitably, I asked him if he could not utilize that same principle to be delivered from his own morbid obesity, which was a much more serious threat to his health than my cold was to mine. He explained that there was a difference: his obesity was the result of his own sinful choices, whereas my cold was an attack from without, from Satan. My cold was therefore "covered" by the blood of Christ and his obesity wasn't. I didn't pursue it further, but if I had I could have pointed out that Christ also bore our transgressions on the cross, and by his own logic he was implying that Christ did not die for whatever sins had led to his obesity.

Christians do get sick. Sometimes even heroic faith

does not bring healing. So the adherents of the faith-claim theology are constantly trying to clean up logically after themselves. But the faith-claim teaching does spring from a truth – as most heresies do – even though it takes that truth in the wrong direction. The New Testament itself sees the fulfillment of Isaiah 53 in the healing ministry of Jesus: "They brought to him many who were demon possessed, and he cast out the spirits with a word, and healed all who were ill, in order that what was spoken through Isaiah the prophet might be fulfilled, saying, 'He himself took our infirmities and carried away all our diseases'." (Matthew 8:16-17)

If Jesus healed them as the fulfillment of prophecy, why not us? If Jesus bore our sicknesses to take them away, why do we still bear them? The attraction of the faith-claim teaching to people with debilitating illnesses, chronic pain, and incurable conditions, is obvious; our hearts must melt with compassion, as Jesus' did, at the overwhelming reality of human pain and suffering. And if we have a way to relieve that suffering, we must.

But the simple, cause and effect logic of the faith-claim teaching does not stand up to logical or biblical scrutiny. The New Testament teaching is considerably more complex.

The big fallacy of the faith-claim teaching

The most glaring fallacy of the faith-claim teaching is so huge, so obnoxiously obvious, that it's hard to see. It is this. If Jesus takes away all the preliminary disintegrations of the body (sickness), then why doesn't he take away the final disintegration of the body (death)? For Jesus certainly died to save us from death as much as he died to save us from sickness! Why do Christians die at all? What good is it, really, to be – as my friend wanted me to be – sniffle-free my whole life if I'm going to drop dead at the end of it like everyone else? The faith-claim teaching is like telling a death row inmate that he's been released from his cell but that he still has to go back at the appointed time for his execution. Small consolation. Sickness and death are part of the same curse. The real problem is not sickness, but death, of which sickness is just a herald, and our real need is not freedom from the discomforts of illness, but freedom from death. We need, not so much healing as resurrection.

But Jesus did heal people. What does that mean?

Jesus healed: why?

We must remember, to begin with, that the people of Jesus' day were still living substantially under the old covenant, the law of Moses, which was not rendered obsolete until Jesus died on the cross. And Jesus did his earthly work among the Jews under the structure of the law of Moses. The connection of sickness and punishment still existed, as is evident in Jesus' healing of the paralytic, to whom Jesus said first, "Son, your sins are forgiven you" (Mark 2:5). To the crippled man whom Jesus had healed by the pool of Bethesda, Jesus said, "See, you have been healed; sin no more, lest something worse come upon you" (John 5:14). Many of the Jews that Jesus healed were in fact sick because of their sins. This was not true in every case – the man born blind was not being punished for his own or his parents' sins (John 9:2-3) – but it was probably true in most cases, and the healing miracles of Jesus were on this

37

background part of the gospel proclamation of the coming of a new covenant and the free forgiveness of sins.

Jesus' healings were not only a conquest of sin and guilt but also an assault on the demonic kingdom. The gospels tear aside the veil of invisibility and reveal the demonic activity that often lies at the root of human bodily ills. Sometimes, to heal people Jesus had to first exorcise demons. This is not to suggest that every sickness is demonic in nature, but simply that where it is, Jesus has sovereign power to relieve it. This is a truth that requires extreme care in its application – a care that my obese friend did not exercise when he told me that my cold was demonic. Still, we have no reason to deny that some of what is wrong with the bodies of humans, in general, is demonic. Perhaps it is beyond our wisdom, apart from special revelation, to know exactly how and where Satanic power impinges on our physical lives. Paul knew his "thorn in the flesh" to be a "messenger from Satan," but this does not mean that Paul was demon possessed. Perhaps we can only say in a general way that the spiritual warfare between the kingdom of Christ and the kingdom of Satan does have our bodies as one of its battlefields. Jesus' healings and exorcisms demonstrate that he has the victory in this warfare.

Jesus' healings also had a special historical function. They served to identify him as the divine Son of God, the promised Messiah : "Then the eyes of the blind shall be opened, and the ears of the deaf shall be unstopped" (Isaiah 35:5, quoted in Matthew 11:5). They served to bear witness that the purpose of Jesus' coming and kingdom was to bring life and to erase all the effects of sin and death. But the healing miracles were not the fullness of the kingdom. The people healed by Jesus, and even those brought back from the dead by Jesus, got sick again and eventually died. To take the healing activity of Jesus as the pattern for normal Christian existence after Jesus died and rose and returned to his Father is to misconstrue its purpose completely. The healings were but signs of the more complete and perfect physical redemption that Jesus came to provide for believers. In the New Testament, it is not Jesus' healings but Jesus' own resurrection to glory that is the "first fruits," the real beginning of the consummated kingdom.

The healing miracles of Jesus do not mean that Christians should not be sick. They do mean that Jesus has come to make complete conquest of sickness, on his own timetable. They point to something else. They point to resurrection.

What to think when you get sick

As believers wait for resurrection, we continue to get sick. How are we to think about this?

Emphatically not as the Israelites under the law thought about it, for something has changed completely and forever with the sacrificial death of Jesus Christ in our place. Jesus took all of God's wrath, punishment, and curse for those whom he represented on the cross. "There is therefore now no condemnation for those who are in Christ Jesus" (Romans 8:1). So the old equation of sickness and punishment is obsolete for those who believe in Christ. "I am sick, so God must be punishing me" is an instinctive thought, but for a Christian it is false. Just as false, for reasons we have suggested, is the thought, "I am sick, so I must not have enough faith." But if sickness is not punishment, or the fruit of unbelief, what is it?

39

Sometimes in the New Testament sickness is a method of divine discipline. Discipline is fundamentally a different thing from punishment: the goal of punishment is justice and retribution, while the goal of discipline is the growth and good of the person disciplined. Paul explains to the Corinthians that some of them were "weak and sick" because of their flippancy in the celebration of the Lord's Supper. Indeed, some had even died for the same reason. This is hard discipline, but it is clear in the passage that it is discipline; even though Paul uses the word "judgment" (which could mean punishment), his explanation shows that it is discipline he has in mind: "But when we are judged, we are disciplined by the Lord in order that we might not be condemned along with the world" (I Corinthians 11:32). The illnesses and the untimely deaths in Corinth were visited upon them by God to bring them to conviction and repentance. Paul himself knew this experience. His "thorn in the flesh" was a specific physical ailment – the word "weakness" which he uses in I Cor. 12:9-10 is one of the Greek words for sickness – which was not a punishment but which God refused to remove. And Paul asked the New Testament question: "I am sick, so what is God trying to teach me?" This is what the Corinthians were supposed to ask. The answer, for Paul, was humility and dependence upon the grace of God.

Is God trying to teach me something? That is the New Testament response to sickness. It is important, however, to realize that what God is teaching may not have to do with any specific situation or sin but simply with the believer's need to trust in God's grace and to hope for the complete redemption of the body. "While we are in this tent, we groan, being burdened . . ." (II Corinthians 5:14).

"We ourselves, having the firstfruits of the Spirit, even we ourselves groan within ourselves, waiting eagerly for our adoption as sons, the redemption of our body" (Romans 8:23). Sickness and bodily weakness are simply signs that our redemption is still incomplete, that we must live in hope. If God were to remove all bodily ills from the lives of believers, what would happen to the gospel of Jesus Christ? It would probably be perverted beyond all recognition. The world would want it for the same reason that the world now wants vitamins and health spas and diet pills, and for the same reason that the crowds followed Jesus after he fed them. The focus would shift from eternal life, and from resurrection life, to the extension and enhancement of this physical life. The gospel of Jesus Christ would not be far from the gospel of Jenny Craig.

So God subdues us, as he did Job, and as he did Paul, with continuing reminders that we live in and are part of a fallen, dying, decaying creation.

What to do when you get sick

What do we do about sickness?

We pray. It is absolutely legitimate to ask God for healing, as Paul asked God to remove his malady (II Corinthians 12:8). God does, in his own good pleasure, display his power in the healing of bodies. But we must be prepared also for the answer that Paul received from God, which was that it was not God's will to heal him but to give him the grace to endure. The simplistic view of the faith-claim doctrine, that the failure to be healed is the result of insufficient faith, trespasses violently on the sovereignty of God and lands the poor sick believer in a psychological

41

torture chamber; not only is he physically sick, but he thinks that he doesn't really believe God's word and promise.

We also use all natural means available to us to alleviate and to cure sickness. There is no biblical mandate to endure sickness and pain passively. As creatures in a dying world, we are engaged in a warfare across the board with death and decay. It is – temporarily – a lost war, but we must fight it anyway. Paul's companion Luke was a physician, and is spoken of honorably as such (Colossians 4:14). The Philippian jailer dressed the wounds of Paul and Silas in his home (Acts 16:33). Paul advised Timothy, who was probably suffering from some kind of digestive ailment, to use a little wine for his stomach. If the faith-claim teaching were true, or if God intended us to suffer passively under bodily ills, these passages would not stand written.

What about the gift of "healing" referred to in I Corinthians 12 as one of the gifts of the Spirit? To deal with this question in depth would take us into a larger discussion of the continuation of the so-called "extraordinary" gifts (tongues, interpretation of tongues, miracles, healing, etc.), which is beyond the scope of this study of the body. It will suffice here to say this: If a gift of healing is currently being given to Christians, it corresponds neither to the kind of plenary healing power seen in Jesus and the apostles, in which case there would have been no "sick and weak" in Corinth, nor to the practices of the "faith healers" of our media, whose techniques are, at best, mass psychology and, at worst, trickery. The Christian with the gift of healing would be, simply, a believer through whom God works to an unusual degree to bestow supernatural healing on the sick. This person would not be able to infallibly heal the sick, and would acknowledge the sovereignty of God, and

42

would know how to accept a "no" from God without blaming the faith of the sick person.

Penicillin, prayer, and the gift of healing notwithstanding, the believer will still experience sickness in this life. In response to this, he should try to get well, and he should try to learn God's lesson, and he should rest in the will of God, and he should long for the complete redemption of his body. For sickness is not just an inconvenience. It is a portent of death.

CHAPTER 4

The Outer Man Decays: Aging

We suggested earlier that modern men would be surprised at the prevalence of sickness in pre-modern societies. For their part, pre-modern men would be surprised at how old we get, and at how many old people there are in modern societies. To the people of Jesus' day, reaching 70 in good health, retiring from work – that is, expecting to arrive at a point in life when one can quit working and still eat (compare Paul's blunt statement, "If a man will not work, neither let him eat," in II Thessalonians 3:10) – and dying of "old age" would be strange and marvelous things. The people who witnessed Peter's healing of a crippled man were amazed at the miracle, not least because "the man was more than forty years old on whom this miracle of healing had been performed" (Acts 4:22). He was, in fact, by the standards of the first century, an old man. And what God had done in his body was not only the reversal of an abnormality but the turning back of the clock.

In the world of the Bible, few people got very old. Nobody really "retired." Aging was not a big issue. But modern medicine has given us aging as an issue. To a large extent, we have traded in the ancient enemy sickness for the newcomer aging. The great fear for most of us is not death by a sudden epidemic or infection, but growing old and feeble. Congestive heart failure has replaced smallpox; crippling arthritis, typhus; Alzheimer's, the bubonic plague.

Because of this historical situation, the teaching of the Bible on aging does not meet us with the same kind of grainy, real life detail as does the teaching of the Bible on sickness. Rather, what we find are generalities and principles. In the end, we find that aging, like sickness, is simply death already at work in the body.

It should be emphasized too that our interest here is not in what the Bible says about old age, and older persons, in general. If it were, we would have to say much about the special position of social dignity that the Bible assigns to the aged (for example, in places like Leviticus 19:32 and I Timothy 5:1). We would have to say something about the provision for the care of the elderly (for example, the "widow's list" of I Timothy). And we would have to emphasize that growing older in years should be, for a Christian, a holy process of becoming more like Christ. Older Christians should be persons of deeper faith, greater love, and more vibrant hope than younger Christians. The news about aging, viewed in its biblical totality, is not all bad.

But our topic is the body, and the aging of the body. Here, indeed, the news is not good.

The biblical vocabulary for aging

Where our contemporary vocabulary about aging is

rich, due to the prominence of the topic in our lives, the Bible's is meager. And where our vocabulary tends to view aging in terms of the mere passage of time (aging, older, elderly), the Bible's tends to view aging in terms of the effect of the passage of time on the body. The Hebrew of the Old Testament has no distinctive verb "to grow old," but only a multipurpose verb which can mean not only to "to grow old" but also "to decay," "to waste away," or "to disintegrate." It is often difficult to know exactly when the word is referring specifically to aging. David says, "When I kept silent about my sin, my bones *grew old* through my groaning all day long" (Psalm 32:3); Job says, "I am *growing old* like a rotten thing, like a garment that is moth eaten" (Job 13:28). Both David and Job were experiencing what felt to them like an accelerated process of aging, which was closely connected to the dissolution of the body that ends in death.

The Greek of the New Testament has a similar word that denotes a process of corruption and disintegration. It can refer to the gradual destruction of simple things, such as what happens to a wool garment when the moths eat away at it (Luke 12:33). It can refer metaphorically to moral corruption: "Bad company *corrupts* good morals" (I Corinthians 15:33). It can describe destruction in general, as in the divine threat that "if any man *destroys* the temple of God [which here is the church], God will *destroy* him" (I Corinthians 3:17). And it can describe what happens to the human body at death. "You will not allow your holy one to see *corruption*" (Acts 2:27; 13:35); this is the prophecy that God will rescue Jesus from the grave before his body decays. When the present body dies, "it is sown in *corruption*" (I Corinthians 15:42).

46

The same word is used, in two significant contexts, to denote what is happening to our bodies right now. "Though our outer man is decaying, our inner man is being renewed day by day" (II Corinthians 4:16). This statement encapsulates, in the two phrases "inner man" and "outer man," the Bible's doctrine of man as a complex unity: there is a man which cannot be seen, and there is the physical man which can be seen, and both are "man." The "outer man" is the body. And there is a double process taking place in the life of the Christian: the inner man, the soul or spirit, is moving towards likeness with Christ, while the outer man, the body, is decaying. It is significant that Paul uses the word "decay," which, as we've seen, can apply to physical death, to describe what is presently happening to the believer's body. The decomposition of death has already begun.

This can only mean aging. It is true that Paul's body was also subjected to abuse and violence for the sake of Christ (II Corinthians 11:23-27). But beatings and stonings are not decay. Decay is something that works from within. Paul recognized the slow, inexorable deterioration of his body and knew that death was already at work.

But Paul, who always looked for the "big picture," saw the living corruption of the human body as part of the larger corruption of the entire creation. "The creation itself will be set free from its slavery to *corruption* into the freedom of the glory of the children of God. For we know that the whole creation groans and suffers the pains of childbirth together until now. And not only this, but also we ourselves groan within ourselves, waiting eagerly for our adoption as sons, the redemption of our body" (Romans 8:21-23). The canvas in this passage is a cosmic one. The whole creation is aging, dying, sinking into terminal decay; the whole creation is groaning, both with pain and with longing for the day when this process of corruption will be radically reversed; believers, as creatures in the fabric of the present creation, look at their dying bodies and at the rotting edifice of the first creation, and we too groan and hope. Our hope for ourselves is the redemption of the body, the resurrection. And our hope for the creation is that it will be renewed, that it will be a new heavens and earth one day.

For now, we grow old. Even apart from sudden violence to our bodies, and apart from sickness, we decay. Even the person in perfect health is decaying.

The stages of decay

Let us set before our minds' eyes three bodies. The first is the body of a 25 year old professional athlete, in the prime of life; the second is the body of a 90 year old woman, near death; the third is the body of a dead person in the grave. In terms of appearance, there are vast and obvious differences among the three bodies. The dead body may be little more than dust. In terms of function, there are again large differences: the athlete's body moves with speed and power, the woman's body moves slowly and painfully, and the dead body moves not at all. But theologically, these three bodies are identical. They are all under the power of corruption. The athlete is dying just as surely as the old woman, and both athlete and woman will end up in graves.

Prime, decline, and dissolution are but three stages of the death that the body dies. As I write this, I am 52. As I survey the "tree" of my own family, I can see the stages. My two grandchildren are one and three; they are soft and flexible and getting larger and stronger by the day. My children, all in their twenties, are in the prime of power and beauty. My parents, in their seventies, are weakening dramatically; my mother is under the clear death sentence of Alzheimer's. As for me, I still feel reasonably well and am healthy. But death is stalking me from a distance, like a sniper behind a rock, and has wounded me in several places. All of us are dying.

How long? Euthanasia?

Our society, as I write (2003), is headed for a social and financial meltdown. Tens of millions of middle aged adults are headed into retirement and old age. We will retire earlier than any generation before us; we will live longer than any generation before us; the things that eventually kill us will be astronomically more expensive than the society in its present form will be able to pay for. And the question will open up: how long should we keep these people alive?

As a society, we will almost certainly become more open to euthanasia. Euthanasia is wrong, and Christians will have to stand against the tide – as we have done with abortion – on the grounds that bodily life is only God's to intentionally take. But as we oppose euthanasia, we should be careful not to slip into materialism through the back door. Materialism sees bodily life as the only life, and therefore as the absolute good, and materialistic philosophy and emotions are behind the modern frantic medical quest to extend bodily life by all possible means, no matter how expensive. That's why many of my generation will live too long, and become a burden on their families and society.

49

Euthanasia is also a materialistic implication: our society's materialistic majority will begin seriously considering euthanasia when the negative impact of longer lives on the present quality of life begins to outweigh the benefits of longer lives. In other words, when the support of slowly dying baby boomers begins to make miserable the lives of those still working – higher taxes, reduction of leisure, stress – then the society will do something drastic about it.

Morally, it will be despicable when doctors, legislators, judges, and sons and daughters begin deciding when older people will die. But let us not, as Christians, oppose this for the wrong reasons. Bodily life is not the ultimate value. We should be as much against the mindless and expensive extension of bodily life as we are against euthanasia; both are idolatrous. If I die at 75 at the hands of a government-empowered doctor, it's not a lot different *for me* than dying at 80 of disease. It's different for the doctor: he's a murderer. I'll protest, and then I'll go meet Jesus. Those five years are not an absolute good.

We will oppose euthanasia because it destroys the souls of those who do it, not because we think so highly of our own lives. And we will refuse to extend our own lives through artificial, expensive, and unreasonable means. The body is going to grow old, and it's going to die of something no matter what we do.

A young body is better than an old body

In spite of the fact that humans in all stages of physical life are dying, young bodies are better than old bodies. I would not trade in my 52 year old mind for the mind of a 20 year old. Horrors! But I'd trade in my 52 year old body for my 20 year old body in a second.

The ideal of a youthful body dominates our culture. Industries like cosmetics, nutrition, and medicine strive to retain or recapture youthful strength and beauty. The hottest athletes and entertainers are young, or older persons who look young. It is true that older people have compensating advantages like wealth and experience and voting power, but even the ideal of the "senior" lifestyle is one that mimics youthfulness.

Now there is much that is perverted and sinful about this idealization of youthfulness. To the extent that it devalues older persons, it is wicked. When it contributes to the notion that older persons cannot be happy, productive, or useful – whether in society or in the church – then it is wicked. (It should be said, in fairness, that older people bring a certain amount of disregard upon themselves by "retiring" earlier and earlier, which contributes to the general feeling that only young people are fit or willing to work.) Society and church are impoverished when the wisdom, knowledge, and experience of older people are disregarded. There is certainly such a thing as age-ism.

But after the proper criticism has been made, there remains a hard, irreducible kernel of truth in the idealization of youthfulness, and it has to do with the body. Young bodies are healthier, stronger, and more beautiful than old bodies. While certain improvements can be made in the short run – heart surgery may mean that an "older" body is actually stronger than a "younger" one, and plastic surgery may mean that an "older" body is more attractive than a relatively "younger" one – the fact remains that over the long haul, the body weakens and wrinkles. Aging can be slowed, temporarily detoured, but it can never be reversed

51

or stopped.

And let us be honest here. There is something undeniably tragic about what happens to the body in aging. That it happens in tiny increments makes it easier to bear than sudden injury. But it is still sad. Our nursing homes are filled with the broken, dying bodies of men who once worked sun-up to sundown, and sweated and toiled, and built things, and fought wars, and fathered children, and dreamed lustily about women. With them are the old women, who once bore children, and kept house, and glowed with beauty, and set men dreaming. The strength and beauty are gone. There is only the bare principle of bodily life left; very little of what their bodies were meant to do can now be done. It is true that these older persons, weak in body, may have luminous, glorious souls, especially if they have walked with Christ for many years. But the decline of the body is nevertheless a sad thing. We know this. To deny it is shallow.

The health and fitness industry, the cosmetics industry, the medical industry, and the advertising industry are all bearing their own kind of grudging witness to the truth which the Bible states bluntly: the outer man decays. In these tents we groan. Nobody really wants to grow old in body. We know that aging is death already at work. It is not, as the materialist says, a natural process which we ought to graciously embrace. It is not, as the platonist hopes, the retreating of the shell that imprisons the soul. It is my own death taking place before my very eyes. And as I watch myself die, I groan, and I hope for the resurrection, as the aging, anonymous psalmist did: "You, who have shown me many troubles and distresses, will revive me again, and will bring me up again from the depths of the earth" (Psalm

52

71:20).

That must be the hope and prayer of every aging, dying believer, whether 20 or 90.

Resurrection is a hope rooted in the life, death, and resurrection of Jesus, and it is to Jesus that we must now turn our attention.

CHAPTER 5

The Body of Jesus

The Bible's doctrine of the human body is framed by the three great themes of creation, death, and resurrection. From this point onward, our theme is resurrection. Even the final chapters on Christian living in the body will be an unfolding of the doctrine of resurrection. And, since the resurrection of Jesus' body is the pattern for the resurrection of the believer's body, we begin with a close look at the body of Jesus itself.

Getting the right hope

As we try to understand the biblical doctrine of resurrection, we will have to come to grips with the platonism that has made its way into evangelical piety and thinking. As a matter of practical, everyday faith, the focus of the typical American evangelical Christian's hope is not the resurrection of the body but the "intermediate state," the presence of the soul with Christ which begins at death. Instead of looking for the day when "in my flesh I shall see God" (Job 19:26), most Christians look for the day of death and going away to be with Jesus in heaven. Instead of longing for the day of Christ's coming, most Christians long for the day of their own departure. Content with the appetizer of leaving our bodies and the earth that God created for our habitation behind, we miss the main course of the redemption of the body and of creation. Fixated on the prospect of escape, we forget that Christ's agenda is conquest. We sing about the "salvation of the soul" and "crossing Jordan" and winging our soulish flight to heaven – that is, of death – but all too seldom do we sing about the coming forth of our bodies from the ground at the sound of the trumpet. This emphasis is the telltale fruit of platonism.

The intermediate state, about which we will have more to say, is a biblical thing and a wonderful comfort. But it is not the final redemption. For when Christ purchased believers on the cross, he purchased them in their wholeness, to restore them to wholeness. That means the resurrection of the body.

To make the transition from our death to our resurrection, we must go back to the experience and accomplishment of Jesus Christ, who died and rose. In this, as in everything else that concerns salvation and life, Jesus is the pioneer, the one who treads and clears the path before us.

We will see, first, that the pre-resurrection body of Jesus, that is, the body of Jesus from the moment of his conception in the womb of Mary to the moment of his resurrection, was *a body like our present bodies*. The word "present" is crucial in this statement; the physical existence that Jesus received from his mother Mary was in every way like hers (because it was hers) and like ours: fallen, vitiated, death-laden. This truth can be derived from the New

Testament both through clear doctrinal statements and through observation of Jesus' earthly life.

Jesus had a body like ours

The New Testament writers, as they describe the true humanity of Jesus, do not hesitate to use the word "flesh" (*sarx*), in spite of the fact that this word is loaded with negative moral connotations. Often in the New Testament, "flesh" denotes not merely the physical body, but the entire human nature in its fallenness. Note, for example, that the "works of the flesh" (Galatians 5:19-21) are predominantly sins of the emotions and the mind. Yet Paul boldly declares that Jesus Christ was "revealed in the flesh" (I Timothy 3:16). And, in a chapter which states that "those who are in the flesh cannot please God" (Romans 8:8), the apostle teaches that God sent "his own Son in the likeness of sinful flesh" (Romans 8:3). An astonishing dictum: Jesus was sinful flesh! And, in the gospel which declares that "that which is born of the flesh is flesh and that which is born of the Spirit is spirit" (John 3:6), comes the glorious good news that "the Word [Jesus] became flesh and dwelt among us" (John 1:14).

There is another, flatter Greek word readily available: "body" (*soma*). It is striking, then, that the New Testament writers prefer the stronger, ethically dynamic word "flesh," even at the risk of seeming to class Jesus with sinners. The New Testament is absolutely clear that Jesus never committed sin (John 8:46; Acts 3:14; II Corinthians 5:21; Hebrews 7:26-2; I Peter 1:19; 2:22). His hands, his tongue, his mind, his emotions, and his motives were sinless. There was no remote corner of his life that was not given in complete obedience and consecration to God the Father. He was perfect. So, clearly, when the same writers who declare him sinless also declare him to be "flesh," they do not intend to class him with sinners. Rather, they intend to identify him with a sinful race, to place him in it, as part of it, sharing its liability to curse and death, feeling its woe, and being a man with a body of death.

Admittedly, we stand before an enormous mystery here, and language fails us. Yet something crucial is at stake: the true humanity of Jesus, without which his work of obedience and sacrifice is meaningless for us. The word "flesh" prevents us from diluting or compromising Christ's true humanity. If the New Testament said merely that Jesus had a "body," a *soma*, then we might conclude that he has a physical form, but we might hesitate to conclude that he was true man. We might even reason that a perfectly sinless man could not have a body like ours, and that his body must be a different kind of body. The comic book hero Superman has a body, to be sure, but a body that flies and repels bullets is not a true human body. How could a man who never lusted have a body like mine? But the Bible's use of the strong word "flesh," as applied to the body and human nature of Christ, prevents this heresy. It tells me that his humanity was like mine, and that his moral perfection, achieved in a body like mine, was perhaps the most staggering human achievement of the ages; that temptations were not just formalities for him (like bullets off of Superman's chest), but deadly threats to his mission and my salvation; that Jesus went through a normal childhood without ever dishonoring his parents, through a normal adolescence without lust, and through an adult career filled with adulation and attention without even a flickering of sinful pride.

Jesus' pre-resurrection body was exactly like ours. If this truth is qualified or compromised, we lose the Jesus who can deliver from sin and death: "Since then the children share in flesh and blood [human bodily existence], he himself also likewise shared in the same . . . he had to be made like his brother in all things" (Hebrews 2:14, 17). The evidence from the gospels supports this.

To say this another way, Jesus in his human nature was *nefesh hayah*, a living creature. His humanity came – as ours – from the ground, through Adam, by way of Mary, the daughter of Adam.

Jesus experienced bodily life as we do

Jesus was born exactly as I was, through the same hard process of labor and childbirth, the process which had been cursed with pain after the fall (Genesis 3:16). His conception was a miracle; his birth was entirely normal.

He grew exactly as I grew, in "stature" (Luke 2:52). He did not come forth into the world as some strange, tiny version of an adult, but as a true baby. Toddling, potty training, and bumps and bruises were his lot. His mother never had to discipline him for rebellion or defiance, but certainly our Lord received the discipline of instruction as Mary and Joseph taught him, probably with swats as well as with other warnings, not to touch fire or to run in front of horses in the street. His growth in stature, in other words, involved not only the growth of his limbs and dimensions but also the normal growth of his brain. He had to learn to talk. He had to learn the Hebrew Scriptures along with the other boys in Nazareth.

The body of Jesus was on the same life to death cycle

as mine, as ours. He began his public ministry at the age of thirty, already an aging man by the standards of the day, and, had crucifixion not intervened, his body would have grown old and died, of some cause, as ours.

When Jesus did not have adequate food and drink, he became hungry (Matthew 4:2) and thirsty (John 4:7; 19:28). He fasted for forty days in the wilderness – can a real human body do this? Of course not; there was certainly supernatural sustenance involved in Jesus' ability to live without food or water for forty days, just as there had been when Elijah went without food for forty days (I Kings 19:8) and when Moses went without food or water for forty days (Exodus 34:28). Jesus' body was subjected to severe hunger in the wilderness, and this trauma made him all the more susceptible to the devil's temptations when they came. The whole temptation event would be meaningless if the body of Jesus were not like ours.

Jesus' body became tired (John 4:6), and it needed sleep (Matthew 8:24). It should be some comfort to know that our Lord knows what it feels like to want to stay in bed. He certainly had his days of energy and his days of lethargy, and – as we've already seen from Isaiah 53 – he was not a stranger to sickness.

Our Lord was also subject to the physical effects of stress. Luke, the physician, notes in his gospel that as Jesus prayed in Gethsemane "his sweat became like drops of blood, falling down upon the ground" (Luke 22:44). Luke is not saying here that Jesus was literally sweating blood but that he was sweating profusely under the severe psychic agitation of the prospect of the cross. The connection of mind and body was for Jesus the same as it is for us. The instinct to survive, to protect the body from pain, to shrink

59

from danger, was as powerful in him as it is in us. And when this deep human instinct collided with the holy will of Jesus to perform the task given to him by the Father, the result was what Luke calls "agony," and its somatic expression was profuse sweating.

Then, finally, Jesus' body died. We must consider his death for a moment, not from the angle of its theological meaning as atonement for sin, but simply for what it implies about his body. Paul describes our present bodies as "sown [that is, dead and buried] in corruption [decay, un-creation] . . . in dishonor . . . a natural body" (I Corinthians 15:42-44). Our present bodies are characterized by mortality; they die. That Jesus died puts his pre-resurrection body into this same category; it was corruptible, dishonorable [subject to deterioration, mutilation, and destruction], and natural – from the earth, from Adam, from Eve, from Mary. If Jesus had not risen from the dead, his body would have decayed and returned to dust, as the prophecy from Psalm 16:10 implies ("You will not allow your Holy One to see decay," applied to Jesus in Acts 2:31). God rescued Jesus from physical decomposition by raising him from the dead.

Did Jesus' body have supernatural powers?

What about the seemingly supernatural physical powers that Jesus displayed at times? What about, for example, his walking on the water? What about his escapes from seizure by this enemies that seem to go beyond the normal (for example, John 10:39)? What about the transfiguration, during which Jesus' physical appearance became saturated with radiant light? These events are to be regarded, simply, as miracles. When Jesus walked on the

60

water, it was not because his body was different, but because gravity was miraculously superseded; remember that Peter also walked on the water. It was no different in principle from the miracle of the floating axehead (II Kings 6:6). God's miraculous power broke into the physical life of Jesus just as it did for many others within the scope of his ministry. This does not mean that his body was different from ours.

Let us sum up what has been said about the pre-resurrection body of Jesus like this: *what we are in body, Jesus became.*

But that he did not remain.

Jesus' resurrection body: the same, real body

There is much fuzzy thinking about the resurrection body of Jesus. The most serious heresy, which goes back to the early centuries of the church and is still propounded today by the Jehovah's Witnesses, is that Jesus rose from the dead in some spiritual sense but not in body. Akin to this, with a modern flavor, is the liberal theological talk about the "Easter faith of the church" instead of the resurrection of Christ, which reduces the resurrection of Christ to an event which happened in the hearts and thoughts of the early Christians but not necessarily in real history. Are the bones of Jesus still lying somewhere in Israel? To this question, the Watchtower Society answers yes, and the modern liberal theologians answer that it doesn't really matter as long as the church believes that he rose, which is simply superstition.

The witness of the New Testament is clear: the body of Jesus came forth alive from the grave of Joseph of Arimathea, and is no longer there.

None of the gospels describes the actual resurrection. Nobody witnessed the event. That moment when the stiff, lacerated, embalmed and wrapped corpse of Jesus came to life was a private one, shared only among the members of the Trinity. Only after he came out did witnesses see him. Luke places the risen Jesus first on the Emmaus road, walking and talking with two of his followers (Luke 24:13 ff). These disciples did not at first recognize him. Why? Luke's explanation is that "their eyes were prevented from recognizing him" (24:16). This implies, however, that Jesus looked like a normal, physical man; if he had been twelve feet tall, or if he had been clothed with heavenly splendor, or if he had had a halo over his head, they would not have treated him as a mere fellow traveler. He seemed to them as a normal man.

Mary had a similar experience. When she first saw the risen Jesus, she thought that he was the caretaker of the cemetery (John 20:15). Again, it is the ordinariness of Jesus' physical appearance that strikes us in this.

The gospels are clear that the risen body of Jesus was the same body that had died and been buried. After the resurrection, the tomb of Jesus was empty. Cleopas, one of those who walked with Jesus on the Emmaus road, said, "When they were at the tomb early in the morning, they did not find his body" (Luke 24:22-23). So the notion of a "spiritual resurrection" or an "Easter faith" resurrection is one that the original witnesses would find very strange. It was the brute physicality of the resurrection – the emptiness of the tomb, the physical presence of Jesus himself – that shocked, then astonished, then empowered them. Indeed, the human mind is inclined to find any other explanation for the appearance of a previously dead person than physical resurrection: it must be a ghost, it must be a vision, it must be a dream, but it certainly cannot be a resurrection! The disciples themselves, far from being credulous sentimentalists in the process of creating an "Easter faith" resurrection, were skeptical. Thomas demanded to touch the risen body of Christ, and Jesus invited him: "Reach here your finger and see my hands; and reach here your hand, and put it into my side" (John 20:27). In Luke's gospel, the disciples at first think that they are seeing a spirit, a ghost – anything but a real, risen body. Jesus addresses this directly: "See my hands and my feet, that it is I myself; touch me and see, for a spirit does not have flesh and bones, as you see that I have" (Luke 24:39). Flesh and bones. Nothing could more graphically describe a true body. Put your hand into my side. Nothing could more clearly declare that it was the same body that died that was now alive.

Jesus' resurrection body: new and glorious

The risen body of Jesus – the same body that died and was buried – came forth from the grave with new qualities and powers. Luke seems to hint at this when he describes how Jesus "vanished" (24:31) and was suddenly present (24:36). John, too, seems to suggest that Jesus' risen body had unique powers of movement, twice coming to the disciples through locked doors (John 20:19, 26). In the gospel accounts, the superior qualities of Jesus' risen body are muted; Jesus did not spend his last days on earth showing off the powers of his body, but teaching and preparing his disciples to carry on his work after his ascension. It is in the theological passage I Corinthians 15:42-44 that we find some indication of the true measure of the newness of the resurrection body: it is incorruptible, honorable, powerful, and Spiritual. The resurrection body never dies, never grows old or despicable, never weakens, never suffers. It is "Spiritual," not in the sense that it is immaterial, but in the sense that it is completely filled and suffused by the life of the Holy Spirit. In this passage, Paul is speaking of the nature of the future resurrection bodies of Christians, but because he has already argued that the resurrection of Jesus and the resurrection of believers is one connected thing, we are fully justified in applying his description to Jesus' body too.

Jesus is still a man!

One more misunderstanding remains to be addressed. Jesus was a body as he came out from the tomb, and Jesus was a body when he ascended into heaven, and Jesus is still a body as he sits at the right hand of God. Jesus carried his true humanity into heaven and he is still a real man. With a body. Many Christians envision a physical resurrection, and a bodily Jesus with the disciples for forty days, but then they envision, at the ascension, some transformation or dematerialization of the body of Jesus which calls into question his present physical existence. "There is one mediator between God and man, the man Christ Jesus" (I Timothy 2:5). To be fully a man means to have a body.

And Jesus will return from heaven in his body, as the angel explained to the wondering disciples in Acts 1:11.

Our evangelical language about Jesus being "in our hearts" can become careless and platonic. Jesus Christ is with us, indeed, by virtue of his deity – for he is not only

64

true man but also true God! – and by virtue of his Spirit, who is omnipresent and who dwells in the hearts and bodies of believers as the representative of Jesus Christ. Jesus promised to be with us until the end of the present age (Matthew 18:20). At the same time, and in an equally biblical sense, Jesus is not with us. As God incarnate, as the Word who became flesh, he is not with us. We cannot see him, or touch him, because he is not with us but with his Father in heaven. So we long for him, and wait for him.

What we are in body, Jesus became.

What Jesus is now in body, by his resurrection, we who believe in him will become.

CHAPTER 6
The Body to Come

Materialism and platonism both consign the human body to oblivion. It dies and rots and that's the end. There is no future for it. To the extent that Christians have shifted our hope from resurrection to the intermediate state, we have surrendered the theological field to these foes and have given tacit, though unintentional, support to their claim.

We must reclaim the field and proclaim the hope of the resurrection for the fallen, dying, disintegrating bodies of Christians. We must fill the imaginations of believers with the glory of resurrection and with the events of the last day, with the earth giving up the bodies of Abraham, Isaac, Jacob, Deborah, David, and Ezekiel, of Peter and John and Stephen, of the martyrs and the missionaries and reformers and all the faithful members of the true church, and with the instantaneous metamorphosis of the bodies of those saints who live to hear the trumpet sound, and with the vision of the millions of the justified rising through the air toward the descending Christ like iron chips to a great magnet, to meet him and accompany him to the earth that he is about to judge and reclaim. Next to this magnificent biblical panorama, the usual quasi-platonism stuff that passes for future hope in most Christian preaching and conversation today is a poor diet indeed, watery broth in the presence of a prime rib dinner.

The last gasp of platonism in my thinking

Whatever platonism lingered in my own thinking about the human body got rooted out during my last year at seminary. We had heard a prayer request about a fellow student's wife in whose brain a tumor had been found. I regret to say that I didn't pray much about it. I didn't know the student well and I didn't know his wife at all. It seemed far away, and I suppose I thought it would all turn out fine.

Then, not more than a month later, the report came that this young woman was dead. I went into an empty classroom with tangled, violent emotions. I was sad, thinking of the young husband who had so suddenly lost his wife. I was also feeling guilty because I had not thought about her, or prayed. But most of all, I was just angry – not at God, whom I knew to be sovereign and wise, but at death itself, at the affront of it, the ugliness of it. I kept slamming my fist down on a table. I knew that the dead woman's soul was with Jesus, but what really filled my mind in a new way, dormant doctrine springing to life in the face of an enemy, was the hope of the resurrection of the body. It was an outrage that death had made such a claim on the body of a person who belonged to the omnipotent, living Jesus, and it was clear to me that Jesus would have to raise her from the dead, cancer free and death free, to really have the last word and establish his salvation claim. It was that day I learned that a Christian is supposed to be defiant in the face of death.

When I returned the next summer to the church I was serving, I expounded that great resurrection chapter, I Corinthians 15.

No resurrection of the dead?

Some of the Christians in Corinth did not believe in the resurrection of the body. "How do some of you say that there is no resurrection of the dead?" (15:12) We can only infer what the reasons for this error may have been among the Corinthians. There was a bias against the body in Greek thought, which Paul encountered in Athens when he spoke to the "philosophy club" at the Areopagus. The intellectuals there listened to him with some interest until he mentioned the resurrection, and then they scoffed (Acts 17:32). It is likely that something like this same bias was present in Corinth. When Paul raises the question, "But how are the dead raised, and with what kind of a body do they come?" (15:35), he is probably articulating the question of the skeptical platonist, who tries to demonstrate the absurdity of resurrection by pointing out its logical incongruities – is an old person raised old or young? is the ugly person raised ugly or beautiful? and what about the person whose body has been burned, or digested by animals?

The Corinthians probably had a "christianized" version of this aversion to bodily resurrection. They may have believed that the resurrection was something "spiritual," something that took place at conversion and baptism, and something that lay behind the spiritual gifts which they were experiencing with such intensity, a present

68

rather than a future thing. Their thinking might have been: Who needs some crude physical resurrection when we are already enjoying the fullness of resurrection life? In any case, some among them were saying that there is no resurrection of the body.

Paul's irrefutable syllogism

The gospel is not simply logic, but the biblical writers often utilize logic, as Paul does here. In Paul's effort to persuade the Corinthian skeptics of the resurrection of believers' bodies, he employs the well known "syllogism" – if A, and if B, then C.

Paul's "A" is that **Jesus himself rose from the dead.** Paul begins here because he knows that he has the Corinthians' agreement on this point. The resurrection of Jesus was among the things "of first importance" that he preached to them, and through faith in which they were saved. He reminds them of the many witnesses, and of his own witnessing of the risen Christ on the Damascus road.

Paul's "B" is the hinge of the syllogism: **Jesus' resurrection is part of a larger event, the "resurrection of the dead [plural, "dead ones"].** This point occupies vv. 12-19, and is encapsulated by the assertion of 15:16, " . . . for if the dead are not raised, then not even Christ has been raised."

The "C" is the conclusion: **Therefore, if there is no general resurrection of the dead, then not even Christ has been raised and there is no gospel and no salvation.**

And Paul is assuming, hoping with prayer, that the Corinthians will be driven by the force of this unacceptable conclusion to acknowledge that there is a resurrection of the body for Christians.

Behind the syllogism: the unity of Christ and believers

What lies behind the hinge of the syllogism is the doctrine of the unity of believers with Jesus Christ. Christ's resurrection is not an isolated event, but simply one instance – albeit the first in order of time – of a larger, more inclusive resurrection. The wayward Corinthians were treating Jesus' resurrection as the only one of its kind; Paul is saying that it is one of many of its kind!

Paul explains this unity in 15:20 and 23; he compares it to a harvest. In ancient agriculture, grainfields were sown by hand over days, and certain parts of the grain ripened earlier than others. Christ's resurrection is the "firstfruits," that is, the very first ripe grain to be harvested, while believers are the larger harvest that follows. With this analogy, Paul accounts both for the unity of the resurrection (one field of grain) and for the historical sequence (first Christ, then believers).

Another passage which powerfully elucidates this unity is Romans 8:29-30: "For those whom he foreknew, he predestined to be conformed to the image of his Son, that he might be the firstborn among many brethren; and those whom he predestined, he also called; and those whom he called, he also justified; and those whom he justified, he also glorified." Jesus Christ is the goal of predestination; those who are predestined are predestined to be exactly like Jesus Christ. Jesus is the elder brother in the family, the "firstborn," but there will be others like him. And the fact that this likeness involves the resurrection of the body is made certain by the fact that the last step in God's work in

70

the saints is glorification – resurrection. Those who are predestined will be glorified exactly as Jesus was glorified, by the resurrection of their bodies. And this Paul says triumphantly in Philippians 3:20-21: "For our citizenship is in heaven, from which also we eagerly wait for a Savior, the Lord Jesus Christ, who will transform the body of our humble state into conformity with the body of his glory." The raised bodies of believers will be exactly like the raised body of Jesus.

Jesus is one with those who believe in him. We are in him, and he in us. Our destinies are intertwined. What happened to him in his human nature must therefore happen to us; he was raised, and we must be raised. It is because of this bond that Paul is able to argue that a denial of our resurrection is tantamount to a denial of Christ's resurrection. And that amounts to the destruction of the gospel.

The logical fruit of platonism is the destruction of the gospel which proclaims the risen Christ and the hope of risen Christians.

What kind of body is the resurrection body?

But what exactly happens at the resurrection? Isn't there some force, after all, to the query of the Corinthians, "With what kind of body do they come?" It is one thing to believe that Jesus rose from the dead. He was in the grave only three days; his body was still intact; there was evidence of the identity of his body in the wounds of the cross which he showed his disciples. But what about the bodies of the martyrs, scattered to the winds as ashes, digested by the wild animals of the Roman arenas? What about the bodies of Abraham and Job and David, long since disintegrated to dust? And what about age? Will Methusaleh be raised as a man of 969 years, and the small child as a child? The difficulties of envisioning the resurrection multiply when we extend the idea over the entire multitude of the redeemed, which no man can number, and the multitudinous manners of their deaths and dispositions of their bodies.

And what about my cousin David Ericsson, who died in a plane crash in the middle of the Amazon rainforest? It was 1971. He was 18 at the time, a recent Christian, returning from a visit to a mission station in eastern Peru. It was weeks before the crash site was finally located, and by that time all that was left of my cousin was a belt buckle. His body was completely gone, taken by the rain, the heat, and the animals. Yet he belonged to Christ. He was predestined to be conformed to the image of Christ. With what kind of a body will he come?

Paul begins his answer to this question, in I Corinthians 15:35-49, with the words, "You fool!" It is important to understand the reason for this rebuke. It is not stupid to ask about the nature of the resurrection body if behind the question is the firm assumption that it is, indeed, a body, and if the difficulties we encounter are the result of a real, bodily resurrection. There are such difficulties! Paul does not rebuke us for our believing questions. He rebukes the Corinthians because behind their question was skepticism; they thought that the difficulties were absurdities which militated against bodily resurrection. We are not fools if we believe in the resurrection of our bodies and want to understand as much as we can about it.

Paul's answer does not answer all of our questions, but it does give a framework. It is, in substance, the same answer we gave in the previous chapter about the resurrection body of Jesus. The resurrection body is a real body; it is the same body that died; it possesses glorious new qualities and powers. Staying with agriculture, Paul likens it to seed. A seed has one "body," one physical form, when it is sown in the ground and killed. It comes forth from the ground with a new and different "body." But it is still the same organism which was sown. The present body, says Paul, is mortal, weak, dishonorable, and natural; the resurrection body will be immortal, powerful, honorable, and Spiritual (that is, of the Holy Spirit – not ghostly or incorporeal). So we infer that the resurrection body will be free from death, sickness, pain, aging, injury, and exhaustion. We can understand it now mainly by negation: it will not be like the present body in those things which cause us grief and sorrow.

This does not satisfy our curiosity. It simply sets some boundaries. The resurrection body will not be a mere duplicate of the body that dies; we cannot predict things like size, apparent age, appearance, or even the presence of reproductive organs (since in the resurrection there will be no marriage or reproduction, Matthew 22:30). At the same time, the resurrection body will be made by God from the old body, so we cannot simply consign the mortal body to oblivion. The dust of Abraham, the ashes of Polycarp, and the molecules of my cousin's body, which have long since become part of the jungle, are still in God's sight bodies to be raised, bodies that are one with the risen body of Christ. They will be, in a great act of divine power that beggars our imaginations, reconstituted, reanimated, and glorified.

73

It will happen when Christ returns

When? At the return of Jesus Christ. "Each in its own order: Christ the firstfruits, after that those who are Christ's *at his coming*" (I Corinthians 15:23). "For the trumpet will sound, and the dead will be raised imperishable, and we [believers alive at the moment of the second coming] will be changed [transformed directly from the condition of mortality to resurrection without passing through death]" (15:52). The resurrection of the dead will be instantaneous, "in the twinkling of an eye" (15:52).

In the resurrection, a precedence of honor will be given to those Christians who have suffered physical death. "We who are alive and remain until the coming of the Lord shall not precede those who have fallen asleep [died]. For the Lord himself will descend from heaven with a shout, with the voice of the archangel, and with the trumpet of God; and the dead in Christ shall rise first" (I Thessalonians 4:15-16). God in his providence ordains that some of his people will die before the return of Christ, and that others will be alive when it happens, and God in his compassion compensates those who have died by raising them first.

Can we imagine this? The trumpet will sound. Jesus will appear, looming over the earth. He will descend, in his risen body, in power and glory to the earth. He will "bring with him" (I Thessalonians 4:14) the disembodied souls of those who have died in his grace; his command will ring out; bodies and souls will be reunited in the integrity of the whole human person; the dead bodies of his people will come forth from graves, and oceans, and deserts, and jungles, remade, glorious, imperishable, rising from all over the earth to meet the Lord in the air as he comes. Then, the bodies of believers alive on the earth will be transformed directly from the living death of the present bodily life to resurrection power and beauty, and another wave of perfect saints will move through the air towards Christ. The redeemer will finally be together with all of his redeemed, and together they will come to claim the earth that rightly belongs to them, a great, holy host.

Never again will there be sickness, or weakness, or pain, or injury, or growing old, or death. Our bodies will be like Christ's, forever.

In light of this, some things must change.

Restoring the resurrection to its place

Our theology, as expressed in our preaching and Bible teaching and talking, must change in such a way that the resurrection of the body, and not the intermediate state, becomes the focus of Christian hope.

We don't need to abandon or modify the Bible's doctrine of the intermediate state. The New Testament teaches clearly that at death the souls of believers pass immediately into the presence of Jesus Christ (Philippians 1:21-23; II Corinthians 5:6-8). Jesus kept his wonderful promise to the criminal crucified next to him: "Today you will be with me in Paradise" (Luke 23:43). The assurance of immediate fellowship with Christ is a sweet hope and one of the bulwarks that sustains the saints in persecution and tribulation. The doctrine of "soul sleep" – that the soul is simply unconscious from death to the resurrection of the body – which has appeared on the fringes of Christian theology, is foreign to the New Testament. The intermediate state is good news and should continue to be part of our preaching.

But it must not be the focus. The resurrection must be the focus, as it is in the Bible. Only by resurrection is the invasion of death finally and completely turned back; only through resurrection is victory over death complete. Perhaps we can grasp this better by imagining how different the gospel itself would be if it proclaimed only that Jesus' soul was with the Father in heaven, while his body was in the grave, if one of the stops in the "holy land tour" were the grave of Jesus with the body still inside. We don't settle for a dead Jesus. Why do we settle so easily for dead saints?

Getting defiant

Our emotional response to death should fit with our belief in resurrection. It is obvious that the resigned, hopeless grief of the materialist, for whom death is the extinguishing of the person, is inappropriate for Christians in the face of death. Paul explains the resurrection of the body to the Thessalonians so that they will not "grieve as those who have no hope" (I Thessalonians 4:13). It is less obvious to us today that the quiet, stoical acceptance of death which seems so pious is equally inappropriate. The proper Christian response to death should be a mixture of anger, defiance, and joy. Death is, after all, no friend but an enemy. Its achievement is a terrible work of destruction. But because we know that it is only a temporary work, and one that will not only be reversed but overwhelmed by the work of Christ, we can rejoice. Looking ahead to the resurrection, we can shake our fists in the face of death – our own or our Christian friends' – and say with Paul: "Death is swallowed up in victory. O death, where is your victory? O death, where is your sting?" We are the advance paratroopers of a great invasion, who have fallen temporarily into the hands of the enemy, but who can already hear the guns of our main force coming, and who smile.

Reforming the funeral service

I've performed a lot of funerals, and I have mixed feelings about them. On the one hand, I think that the funeral service is one of the essential rituals of life. When death takes a person, those of us who remain need to face it together, say goodbye together, and call out to the Lord together. On the other hand, I find that the content of most of our Christian funerals – what is actually said – tends to be insipid, sentimental, and platonic.

If I die before the trumpet sounds, I want a loud, public funeral. I want the family to gather, and I want my church to gather. I don't want a quiet, private exit.

I want my casket to be open. Many people turn their noses up at this good old custom now, as if it were somehow in bad taste to look at someone's dead body. But I want people to see that I'm dead and to make their peace with that fact. I don't want them to think of me "as I was;" I want them to think that now I'm dead and my soul is with Jesus in heaven and this body upon which they gaze will one day rise.

I want somebody to preach about the resurrection of the dead. Let him say something about the intermediate state, which I will be greatly enjoying as the funeral happens. But let him not dwell on the intermediate state; let him rather proclaim that because I belong to Jesus Christ, who rose from the dead, I too will rise from the dead. I don't want my burial to be the disposal of a piece of organic waste, but the planting of a powerful seed.

If I can listen from heaven, I want to hear some loud and happy songs sung at my own funeral. Maybe it's partly a matter of taste, but I find most "funeral music" to be sentimental and platonic. I want songs of triumph and victory, loud, defiant, strident songs.

> *When this poor lisping stammering tongue*
> *lies silent in the grave,*
> *Then in a nobler, sweeter song*
> *I'll sing thy power to save.*
> **(There is a Fountain Filled With Blood, William Cowper)**

> *That word, above all earthly powers,*
> *no thanks to them abideth.*
> *The Spirit and the gifts are ours*
> *through him who with us sideth.*
> *Let goods and kindred go, this mortal life also,*
> *The body they may kill; God's truth abideth still;*
> *His kingdom is forever.*
> **(A Mighty Fortress Is Our God, Martin Luther)**

Let the congregation look death in his ugly face, the death that has taken me, and the death that will one day take them, and shake their fists in his face through the gospel.

What about cremation?

I am often asked about cremation. The Bible says nothing directly to the topic of cremation, but it does give us a doctrinal scaffolding on which to build a biblical view.

If the body is really the person, and if the body of a believer belongs to Jesus Christ, and if the body has a future in resurrection, then it seems that the intentional destruction of the body through cremation is morally wrong. Intention is the key concept. My body could be burned to ashes, or blown apart in war, and God would still raise it from the dead. Even if I am buried in civilized fashion, my body will eventually return to dust, and God will still raise it from the dead. So the issue is not whether God *can* raise a cremated body from the dead. He *can*. The issue is my own intention, and the fact that by choosing cremation I am making a statement about my own body. To the Christian who says, "I want to be cremated," I pose the question, "Why?"

Because it's not as expensive? If this is the real problem, then I say, let the church help with the burial costs.

Because burial takes up too much space? I think this is silly. There's plenty of room for people to be buried.

I fear that the choice of cremation is often a theological statement about the body, which means: this is not really "me" anymore, I'm in heaven with Jesus, my body doesn't matter anymore so just get rid of it. In other words, I fear that in cremation we have creeping platonism. And it is a historical fact that the pagan Greeks and Romans, who did not believe in the resurrection of the body, cremated their dead, and that one of the ways that the early Christians proclaimed their gospel faith was by burying their dead and treating the dead bodies of the saints as something precious. The disposition of a Christian's dead body is not a theologically neutral thing; the way you do it says much about your theology.

Here is the biblical truth. The dead body of a

believer is still that believer and still belongs to Jesus Christ (I Corinthians 6:20). It is still the temple of the Holy Spirit. It does not belong to the funeral home, or to the surviving relatives, or even to the person who died. It belongs in the most literal sense to Christ. And therefore it is nobody's right – except Christ's – to decide upon its destruction. I have no more right to decide upon the fiery destruction of my body after I'm dead than I do right now; it's not mine. If I cannot, morally, pour gasoline over my living body and set it on fire, then neither can I consign it to an oven after I'm dead. If it is Christ's will to bring it back to dust before he raises it, so be it. It's his.

It seems to me that cremation is either materialistic, or platonic, or an arrogant assumption of the rights of ownership.

New bodies on a new earth

Just as the personal hope of the believer is a glorious new body, so the cosmic hope of the believer is a glorious new earth. "But according to his promise, we are looking for a new heavens and a new earth, in which righteousness dwells" (II Peter 3:13). As Paul says in Romans 8:22-23, we humans groan together with the entire creation, waiting for the day when all of the creation will be set free from corruption, futility, and death.

We were made from the earth. We belong to it. It belongs to us. At this point, again, platonism has conditioned us to think of salvation as an escape from planet earth, precisely where the Bible calls us to hope for salvation as the conquest of earth by its creator, the Son of God, and the inheritance of earth by his allies, his troops, his people.

"The meek will inherit the earth" (Matthew 5:5). The enjoyment of earth and the dominion over earth which God set before Adam and his family, but which was squandered through rebellion, has been redeemed by the Father for his family, the brothers of Christ.

Eternal life, in other words, will be physical life. Bodily life. And earthly life. God does not abandon what he has made; he redeems it and purifies it. He will once more look upon his work and behold, it will be very good. It will be the life of glorious, perfected, whole human beings in a glorious, perfected creation. Beyond that we cannot say much more.

What we are, Jesus became.

What he has become, we will become.

CHAPTER 7

The Perversion of the Appetites

We come, finally, in these last chapters, to the theme of Christian ethics. If it is true that the human being is a spiritual-material unity, and that redemption through Jesus Christ is as much the redemption of the body as it is of the soul, then the Christian ethic must be an ethic of bodily life.

Again we will have to steer a biblical course between materialism and platonism.

Materialism makes Pharisees

Materialism tends to produce a way of thinking that regards bodily behavior as the sum and substance of ethical life. Simply put, what you *do* makes you good. Obedience to God, conformity to his will, consists in observable actions. In the New Testament, the Pharisees came closer than anyone to embodying this idea. The Pharisees were not philosophical materialists, but their ethical system had, by the time of Jesus, come perilously close to a crass materialism. The Pharisees once rebuked Jesus and his followers for ignoring the traditional hand-washing ceremony before meals (Matthew 15:1ff). In response, Jesus unleashed a withering polemic against their belief that eating with unwashed hands made a man morally unclean. Nothing going into a man can make him unclean; only what comes out of his heart can do that.

That ethical purity – or impurity – is a matter of the heart is one of Jesus' central teachings, and one of the central emphases of the entire New Testament. A wicked, selfish, lustful heart cannot be concealed before God by proper, civilized, moral bodily behavior. A man may never commit physical fornication, but if he lusts for a woman "he has already committed adultery with her in his heart" (Matthew 5:28). A man may never lift a weapon to destroy his neighbor, but his anger and his scorn are in God's sight the same as murder (Matthew 5:22). The materialist thinks that what is not public is not sin. But the sinful heart is as public to an all-seeing God as a billboard.

You can tell where Christian ethics have been pervaded by materialism, because there you find a proliferation of extra-biblical prohibitions and taboos. The Pharisees, in their zeal to quarantine the person from sinful behavior, did what they called "fencing the law." They added other laws to God's laws as a buffer zone. If God forbade building a fire on the Sabbath, the Pharisees fenced the law by forbidding the lighting of a candle. This same kind of thing continues to surface in Christian circles. If the Bible forbids premarital sex, then we must forbid dancing because it might lead to sex. If the Bible forbids drunkenness, then we must forbid the use of alcohol altogether. If the Bible forbids gambling, then we should forbid the use of playing cards completely. And so forth. It is legalism to add human laws to the laws of God. It is also materialism.

Platonism makes libertines

It does little good to be set free from Pharisaical materialism into platonic spiritualism. A platonistic ethic focuses on the "heart" to the point of devaluing the conduct of the body. It focuses on motives, attitudes, and feelings and separates these inner things from the deeds of the body. How, after all, in a platonistic world, could the mere external actions of the body be as important as the movements of the soul?

Something like this shows up in the Corinthian correspondence. The Corinthians were into freedom. "All things are lawful" was apparently one of their slogans (I Corinthians 10:23). Going beyond genuine Christian freedom, which liberates the believer from the Mosaic law with its curse and from laws imposed on the conscience by humans, the Corinthians seem to have verged on the doctrine that the believer has been severed altogether from *commandments*. Paul hints at this in I Corinthians 5, where he deals with the case of the church member who was living in a public, incestuous sexual relationship. Of course Paul is concerned with the man's sin. But he seems even more outraged by the cavalier attitude of the church: "And you have become arrogant, and have not mourned instead, in order that the one who has done this deed might be removed from your midst" (I Corinthians 5:2). The Corinthians did not see this sin as a serious sin, nor did they think that it would affect their church. It was, after all, a mere sin of the body. They may not have approved, but they tolerated it. And this casual attitude toward a sexual sin fits perfectly with what the Corinthians were thinking about freedom (all things are lawful) and the body (there is no resurrection of the dead). They ended up, not in Christian freedom, but in moral libertinism, which is just slavery to sin by another name.

If it is ghastly that the Corinthians could wink at incest, it is no less ghastly that contemporary confessing Christians can wink at rampant premarital sex even within the church, and at the consumption of "soft" pornography in movies and sitcoms, and at the galloping gluttony of modern American culture. If we love Jesus in our hearts, it is presumed, such lapses are not so bad. And the track record of the modern evangelical churches in the area of church discipline is just as ghastly as that of Corinth.

Materialism produces an externalistic ethic which devalues motive and faith. Platonism produces a spiritualistic ethic which devalues the deeds of the body. They have in common that they sever man through the middle of his being.

Christ claims the whole human nature, soul and body, for his worship and service. He saves it and he sanctifies it.

The appetites of the body

The claim of Christ on the believer's body does not go uncontested. Indeed, as soon as a sinner repents and Christ's lordship is established over the life of that sinner's body, a ferocious struggle breaks out between Christ and the Holy Spirit, on the one hand, and sin on the other. And sin asserts its power in the body through the appetites.

85

This struggle, it should be carefully noted, is not a struggle between matter and spirit, or between body and soul. That's platonism again. It is a struggle between sin and the Holy Spirit across the whole broad front of the believer's existence, in the thinking, feeling, and choosing of the believer as well as in what he does with his body. It is not the case that the soul is good and the body is bad, but rather that sin wants the whole person, body and soul, and Christ wants the whole person, body and soul.

In the body, sin works through the appetites. An "appetite," as I use it here, is a motive for decision and action that arises *from the body itself*. This is to be distinguished from the participation of the body in decisions and actions that arise from what the Bible calls the "heart," the thought, feeling, and imagination of man. From the heart, for example, comes the sin of slander, which is rooted in pride, envy, and the impulse to raise oneself higher by putting another person lower. When slander arises from the heart, it then comes out through the body, the mouth; the body is enlisted and becomes the instrument of sin. But slander is not an appetite.

It works the other way, too. While the appetites arise from the body, they are not ethically significant simply as physiological things. The appetites place ethical decisions before the mind and will. Just having the appetite is not sinful or righteous; it's what you do about it. So it is crucial to understand, as we talk about the appetites, that we are really talking about how the whole person responds to that particular cluster of ethical issues that arises from the body. The frontier between body and soul is porous; we are continually thinking, deciding, and acting as whole creatures.

God the Creator has "programmed" the body with certain appetites. So there is nothing intrinsically sinful about the appetites, any more than there is anything intrinsically sinful about the body itself. The drive of the body for life, sleep, food, pleasure, and sex is there by God's design, and stands under the evaluation of the Creator as "very good." And there are legitimate ways for the believer to satisfy the appetites of the body. God does not issue a blanket veto on the life of the body; rather, he sets boundaries within which the needs of the body are to be satisfied.

Our problem is that all is not exactly as it was when God surveyed the creation and pronounced it to be very good. Adam and Eve rebelled against their Maker, and judgment and curse fell upon them and us. One part of God's curse is God's abandonment of humans to the tyranny of their own sinfulness, which has implications for the life of the body. The appetites, which were created to serve man, become his idols, that which he serves.

How the appetites become idols

In one of the Bible's most somber and terrifying passages (Romans 1:18-32), the apostle Paul explains how God punishes humans for their idolatry: he turns them over to their idols. Men make idols of created things, preeminently themselves. So, in a judgment of dreadful appropriateness, God "gives them over" (vv. 24, 26, 28) to themselves as gods. And perversion follows. As men have "exchanged" the true God for idols, now they "exchange" the natural sexual relationship between man and woman for homosexuality. This demonstrates the folly of idolatry: these humans, these "gods," can't even figure out which body parts go with which!

This judgment is God's removing of any restraints on the sex appetite, allowing it be become cancerous and twisted, to spill out of the created boundaries. But this can happen with any of the appetites when sin, not God, is lord. We must look honestly and carefully at what happens to the appetites, and to bodily life itself, when sin is in control.

The survival appetite perverted: bodily life as an idol

First and foremost among the appetites is the hunger for life itself, the survival instinct. The desire of the body for life expresses itself physiologically through involuntary responses like shock, fever, and adrenalin bursts. The same appetite can also assert its power at the level of conscious thought and decision.

If we could somehow stand back from human life in the present world and view it as a stranger would, it would strike us how much of the vast sum of human activity is centered on survival. Through most of history this has been more immediately obvious. Recently, industrial and technological societies have managed, for the first time in human history, to free significant numbers of people from concern for daily survival. Most of the readers of this book will be in this category. But those of us who have never unwillingly missed a meal must realize that our lives rest on a huge, complex foundation designed to keep us alive. I am free to write this book because there is lots of food in my house, and more at the supermarket. If any of my next few meals were in doubt, I'd be gardening, or hunting, or foraging, rather than writing.

The appetite to live is created by God. But it is perverted by sin. "Skin for skin! Yes, all that a man has he will give for his life" (Job 2:4). When Satan speaks these words to God he is describing the survival appetite deformed by sin into an idol.

When God in judgment gives man over to live in independence from the Creator, the desire to preserve bodily life is cut off from the desire to love God above all things, and the activity of preserving bodily life is severed from faith in the care and provision of God. So sinful man perceives himself to be alone on the earth; he has no one besides himself in whom to trust; the survival of his body on the earth becomes the first priority; life becomes sweat, and struggle. The earth, and the weather, and the animals and insects, and even other humans, become threats to this quest.

Jesus summarizes the serious questions of survival: "What shall we eat? What shall we drink? With what shall we clothe ourselves?" He adds: "For all these things the Gentiles eagerly seek" (Matthew 5:31-32). The "Gentiles" in this passage are the pagans, those who live outside of a covenant relationship with the true God, and who depend on idols (which are really elements of the creation itself) for their survival. Instead of enjoying life as the gift of the Creator, they are obsessed with life as a possession. They have no peace.

In the affluent industrialized world, we have taken the perversion of this lust for physical life to a new level of sophistication. Feeling free from anxiety about tomorrow's food and drink, we cultivate anxiety about the distant future. We worry about retirement. We buy insurance for future contingencies like aging, disability, and illness. The fear of death never really vanishes. It just recedes, and we chase it as it does.

There is also something perverse in our society's relationship with modern medicine. I don't want to be misunderstood on this point: I consider medicine to be one of the great providential gifts of God, and I rejoice to receive its blessings for myself and my family. But something is out of proportion, and the most obvious symptom of this is the preposterous cost of medical care. If it is true that we show what is most valuable to us by what we are willing to pay for it (or, as Jesus put it, "Where your treasure is, there will your heart be also"), then we are a society which worships bodily life, bodily health, and bodily comfort as a god. Modern doctors are no longer artisans – as they were in pre-modern societies – but aristocrats, demigods who dispense to us what we desire the most, and though we gripe about it, we are willing to pay them what they ask. We pay our doctors more than we pay our president, or our generals, or our teachers. (The only ones we pay better than doctors are our entertainers!)

What is out of proportion is the value that today's "Gentiles" place on sheer bodily life. It is all they think they have. They are mostly materialists. "All that a man has he will give for his life," pronounces the devil over our clinics, hospitals, and pharmaceutical labs.

Someone may object to this that history and experience furnish many examples of people giving up their lives for noble causes. It is true that there are exceptions to Satan's statement, but they are few and far between. Furthermore, when an occasional human gives up his or her bodily life for a cause, the rest of us stand amazed, as if in the presence of a marvelous enigma, because the priority of bodily life is assumed and such a person has acted against this assumption.

The sleep appetite perverted: sloth

The body craves sleep, and the perversion of sleep is sloth. "How long will you lie there, O sluggard? When will you arise from your sleep? A little sleep, a little slumber, a little folding of the hands to rest, and poverty will come upon you like a vagabond, and want like an armed man" (Proverbs 6:9-11). The biblical concept of paradise is not affluent idleness, but productive and joyful activity. Even before the fall, Adam was to cultivate the garden of Eden. To carry out this activity, the body requires sleep. Within the boundaries of a life of productive labor and action, sleep is one of the good gifts of God and is to be enjoyed thankfully and without guilt. Psalm 127:2 chides the workaholics: "It is vain for you to rise up early and go late to rest, eating the bread of anxious toil, for he gives to his beloved sleep."

But man the rebel carries this appetite outside its boundaries and defaces it. It is possible, of course, for a person to actually sleep too much, but that is not really the main problem; the body can only sleep so much. The real perversion of sleep is not too much sleep, but sloth, laziness. It is spending the waking hours, meant for work, worship, and culture, in idleness. Sloth is not just a personality trait, or even a defect. It is a sin. "If anyone will not work, neither let him eat" (II Thessalonians 3:10). This apostolic statement indicts laziness, idleness, unnecessary dependence on the work of others (that is, much of our society's government-supervised redistribution of wealth), and the modern concept of retirement.

A word on retirement is in order here. The idea that a man reaches a point in life when he is entitled to simply stop working and be taken care of by others is unbiblical. Some, it is true – the disabled, the feeble, the sick – should receive "charity" from those of us who can work. But a healthy man, still able to work, still productive, may not biblically leave work for a life of play. He may leave a paying job to do volunteer work, if God has blessed him with the means to do so. But he may not simply retire to the golf course, or to the TV, or to the cruise ship. If he does, he is not entitled to eat, according to Paul.

The appetite for food perverted: gluttony

God created the human body to need food, and he created the earth to provide food. Even after the fall, the earth continues to provide man's food, though man must work much harder now to get this result. It is no sin to eat. It is no sin to eat enough.

Nor, it may be important to add, is it a sin to weave into our eating some beauty, some grace, and some ceremony. When the creatures which are not God's image eat, it is an act of fueling, pure and simple, without reflection or aesthetic pleasure. A dog knows no difference between a garbage scrap and a piece of New York steak; it devours them in exactly the same way, because they're both just fuel. But eating for humans should be more than just fueling. The taste and visual appearance of the things that the Creator has provided for our food should be appreciated. God does not intend for us to live on a naked interface with nature, as animals do. He intends for us to gladly receive what he has provided in the creation and then to apply our own rational and creative powers to it, to make straight boards out of a crooked tree, to spin thread from wool and to make cloth from thread, and, yes, to prepare, cook, season, arrange, and present our food in a way that befits rational beings. A nutritionally sound and savory meal, presented at a lovely table, eaten by people who give thanks to God and enjoy the company of one another – all this is a very human and a very godly thing.

The perversion of the appetite for food is gluttony. When man is severed from God, food becomes one of those created things that man worships for its own sake and serves rather than the Creator (Romans 1:25). One of the characteristics of the enemies of the cross is that "their god is their belly" (Philippians 3:18-19). The appetite has become a lust. Instead of eating to live, as the saying goes, they live to eat.

Gluttony was recognized as a sin also under the old covenant. "For the drunkard and the glutton will come to poverty" (Proverbs 23:21). The law of Moses made provision for defiant and delinquent sons to be turned over to the elders of the community for execution, and one of the parental descriptions of such a son is that "he is a drunkard and a glutton" (Deuteronomy 21:20-21). Drunkenness and gluttony in the Old Testament are twins. They are the same kind of sin.

How strange it is, then, that today's churches and Christians look upon drunkenness with such moral indignation – some even "fencing the law," as the Pharisees did, by insisting on total abstinence – and upon gluttony with such indulgence. Which reader of this book has ever, even once, heard an indictment of gluttony from the pulpit? Here, as perhaps nowhere else, the church is utterly indistinguishable from the world. We eat as much as the heathen do, and the heathen eat too much. Our church potlucks are scenes of gluttony, and we make jokes about eating too much the same way that drunks in the bar make jokes about their drinking. The drunkard, the fornicator, and the brawler are still sinners in our eyes, but the glutton is just, well, a person with a hearty appetite. We even admire those who eat a lot, like the Vandals and the Huns.

Just as the perversion of the sex appetite results in self defacement (homosexuality), so the perversion of the food appetite often results in obesity and early death. There are, of course, some eating disorders that have genuine physiological causes and require medical treatment, and it would not be right to call people who suffer from these "gluttons." But these cases are not the majority. Let us face candidly the fact that the vast majority of people who gluttonize do so because they like it and choose it. And the current epidemic of obesity in America is mostly the result of just eating too much. Repentance may be a difficult road, but repentance – as opposed to "treatment" – is the right road for most of those who eat more than they need to eat. Conveniently, modern humanistic philosophy has redefined gluttony, gutting it (so to speak) of its ethical content and calling it a sickness instead of a sin (as it has done with drunkenness). But this only leaves people helpless, afflicted rather than responsible.

And not all gluttons are fat! It is not being fat that is the sin, but eating more than one needs. A teenager I know is famous for having eaten a hamburger with twelve patties in it. He is tall and skinny, and he may never be fat, but he was – at least at that point in his life – a glutton.

Pleasure perverted: hedonism

The body craves pleasure. It seems to me that generalized physical pleasure must be recognized as an appetite, to be distinguished from the others. Sleep, and eating, and sex are pleasurable, but the body craves pleasure even beyond these needs which are essential for survival and procreation. The most basic manifestation of this appetite is the avoidance of pain and discomfort. The body wants to feel good. Within the boundary of God's commands, this appetite can be satisfied. An aspirin for a headache, a footrub at the end of a long day at work, and a refreshing swim on a hot afternoon are bodily pleasures which, in the context of a whole life lived under the lordship of Christ, can be enjoyed with a good conscience. Jesus certainly enjoyed the footwashing which he received from the sinful woman who came uninvited into the house of Simon the Pharisee (Luke 7:36-50).

But pleasure perverted, emancipated from the Creator's lordship, becomes hedonism – "pleasure-ism." It is difficult to mark a clear line where the legitimate enjoyment of physical pleasure crosses over into hedonism and idolatry. Perhaps the line is somewhat different for each person, according to circumstances. But there must be such a line. A footrub after work is one thing; retaining the services of a full time masseuse is another. When physical pleasure becomes the goal of life; when its pursuit occupies time that should be spent in work, worship, and rest; when its expense becomes unreasonable, then it is crossing over into hedonism and thus into sin. According to the apostle Paul, the people of the last days are "lovers of pleasure rather than lovers of God" (II Timothy 3:4). For such people, pleasure is a Baal.

Besides sleep, food, and sex, what kinds of things can become pleasure Baals?

There is much hedonism in the frenetic pursuit of recreation. Recreation is a complex thing because it serves a variety of needs – mental diversion, social intercourse, and exercise, all legitimate activities within bounds. But there is also, undeniably, a strong component of simple physical pleasure in much modern recreation. Amusement park rides provide the body with thrilling and unusual sensations, as do other "extreme" sports. Between Visalia, where I live, and Los Angeles is one of the meccas of physical thrills, Magic Mountain; you only have to observe the traffic around Magic Mountain on a weekend to understand how seriously Southern Californians take their pleasure. On the same interstate highway that runs by Magic Mountain are other thousands of pleasure seekers on their way to a thousand other places, laden with RVs, canoes, boats, bicycles, motorcycles, ATVs, and jet skis. Los Angeles on Friday afternoon is an enormous pressure cooker that explodes in every direction – north to the mountains, east to the deserts, west to the beaches, south to Mexico – spewing forth its millions in pursuit of pleasure. This is not all sinful and hedonistic. But some of it certainly is, and it is for each person and family to determine where the line lies. We can say, at least, that when such recreations take professing Christians away from their churches on Sunday, these recreations have replaced God.

The abuse of chemical substances also fits into this category of hedonism. People "do" drugs and drink to intoxication because it feels good. In advanced stages of addiction, it is true, the body learns to crave the drug or the

96

alcohol almost as a new appetite in its own right. But it all starts with simple pleasure – the rush, the high, the buzz. It is important to remember in this connection that there is a legitimate use of chemicals for the pleasure of the body; aspirin for pain, novocaine for dental work, or cough syrup (which often contains alcohol) for a cough are all good gifts of God. When the Bible speaks of God's creation of "wine to gladden the heart of man" (Psalm 104:15), there is a recognition that the relaxation caused by a moderate use of alcohol is also a good gift of God. The drink of coffee which picks you up in the morning is, in principle, no different from the glass of wine which relaxes you at night.

The sin does not consist in the use, but in the abuse, of the various chemicals which give pleasure to the body. When the chemical gains mastery, that is, when the chemical compromises reason and responsibility, then there is abuse. This is why drunkenness is a sin. When the desire to use the chemical becomes a compulsion rather than a rational decision – that is, an addiction – then there is abuse. Here again, as with survival and gluttony and sloth, an appetite has become a lust, and something created has become a Baal.

Modern society tends to speak about substance abuse as a "sickness" or a "disease." But the Bible speaks frankly about drunkenness as a sin. Drunkards will not, according to I Corinthians 6:10, inherit the kingdom of God. Alcohol was the only drug available in the ancient world, but we should have no doubt that the same judgments leveled against its abuse extend to the abuse of our modern drugs as well. There are medical dimensions to addictions, and there are times when it is appropriate to treat abusers in hospitals. But the fact remains that substance abuse is fundamentally an ethical problem, and that at some point every addict made a choice to use, and then to abuse, the drug. The tragic and wretched depths to which drug and alcohol addicts can sink are, theologically considered, another manifestation of God turning humans over to the pursuit of their idols. This is how the Drug-Baal and the Alcohol-Baal treat those who worship them! The pleasure appetite perverted comes back on man like a boomerang.

Sex perverted: fornication

Finally, we come to the sex appetite. God has placed within the human body the powerful urge for sexual satisfaction. This appetite serves the purpose of collective "survival" through reproduction, but it also exists and cries out for satisfaction quite apart from any need to reproduce. Sex is not intrinsically the most powerful of the appetites; hunger, and exhaustion, and fear of death completely eclipse it in extreme circumstances. But in a tranquil and affluent society, where food, sleep and survival are not matters of immediate concern, sex will seem like the most powerful and fiery of the appetites.

God has ordained that sexual satisfaction be achieved within the boundary of marriage. The exact boundaries of sloth and gluttony and hedonism may be mushy, but the Creator's sexual boundary is bold and clear. The perversion of the sexual appetite is fornication.

The English word "fornication" translates the Greek *porneia*, which in the New Testament is a general purpose word denoting all sexual activity outside the marriage boundary. The apostles and elders in Jerusalem exhorted the recent Gentile converts to abstain from fornication (Acts 15:20), and Paul, in similar language, states that it is God's will for believers to abstain from fornication (I Thessalonians 4:3). Fornication is a "work of the flesh" according to Galatians 5:19, a manifestation of the entire sinful nature. Fornication includes adultery (Matthew 19:9), incest (I Corinthians 5:1), and sex outside the bounds of marriage. "Because of fornication [that is, in view of the temptation to fornication], let each man have his own wife, and let each woman have her own husband. . . . But if they do not have self control, let them marry; for it is better to marry than to burn" (I Corinthians 7:2, 9). The burning in this passage is not burning in hell but burning with lust, and the premise of the passage is that the satisfaction of the sexual appetite outside of marriage is not an option for a Christian, since marriage is the solution for those who do not have the self control to abstain. "The body is not for fornication," says Paul; fornicators will not inherit the kingdom of God. (I Corinthians 6:9-10).

Beyond fornication, on the far frontier of human depravity, are other perversions of sex: homosexuality (about which we have already heard Paul's verdict in Romans 1), sadism, and bestiality. These practices are not only outside the boundary of the marriage covenant but outside of creation itself. Man in his sexual perversions defies the Creator, despises the creation, and tries to show that he is a god by improving on the Creator's plan. Trying to deify himself, he only defiles himself.

The body is in need of ethical redemption

The human body has fallen under the power of sin along with the whole human person. The body is sinful, not because it is matter, but because it is fallen. The body is not

99

evil, as the platonists think. Rather, it is sinful. Its appetites have been conscripted, twisted, and turned against God. "Wretched man that I am! Who will deliver me from this body of death?" (Romans 7:25)

We have seen already that God will redeem the body from death and destruction through the miracle of resurrection. Now we will see how the Bible brings the power of the resurrection backwards into the present life, and how God in his grace redeems the body of the believer from the tyranny of its own perverted appetites.

CHAPTER 8

Glorify God in Your Body

Jesus Christ lays claim to the believer's body, not only for the future glory, but for present service. "You have been bought with a price; therefore, glorify God in your body" (I Corinthians 6:20).

The materialist's problem is not with "in your body" but with "glorify God." For the materialist, there is nothing outside of the body, nothing except matter, and this stark reality means that all the motives of the man's life turn back on himself. His own life, his own comfort, his own health, his own pleasure. You can't get metaphysics out of physics. The materialist says: glorify yourself, please yourself. The apostle says: glorify God in your body.

When the platonist hears Paul say this, he shakes his head, for he does not believe that the body can be an instrument for the glorification of God. The body is the problem! The body draws the man downward toward his baser nature, and it is only through a process of inner detachment from the body that the man can glorify God. The platonist says: glorify God in spite of your body. The

101

apostle says: glorify God in your body.

Is the body usable?

The platonist's objection is that trying to glorify the pure and transcendent God through the instrumentality of a shriveling, dying material body is absurd. How can the present body, vitiated as it is by death and corruption, sinking by stages toward disintegration, be a fit instrument for the glorification of God? Maybe a risen body, or a different body, could do the job. But not this one!

But the power of the resurrection is already at work in the present life of the Christian. Yes, death works. But resurrection works, too. The reality of sin and death compels us to recognize the mortality of our bodies, but the gospel compels us to evaluate our bodies and our bodily lives in light of the resurrection of Jesus Christ.

Paul's words, "glorify God in your body," are the conclusion of a larger argument in I Corinthians 6 in which he elevates the believer's body to a lofty spiritual dignity. He does this through three definitions of the believer's body: member of Christ, temple of the Spirit, and property of God.

The Christian's body is a member of Christ: union

"Do you not know that your bodies are members of Christ? Shall I then take the members of Christ and make them members of a prostitute? May it never be!" (I Corinthians 6:15)

In the background of this statement is Paul's powerful image of the church as the "body of Christ," on which he elaborates in I Corinthians 12, Romans 12, and

102

Ephesians 4. The relationship between Christ and believers is like that of the head of a body with the rest of the body: the head leads and directs, the parts of the body follow and respond. Now this image of the church and Christ as a "body" is a spiritual, metaphorical image which has to do with unity and variety. What Paul is saying in I Corinthians 6:15 is that the Christian's *physical body* is included in his or her membership in the spiritual body of Christ. The union of Christ with his saved people is a union with *whole* persons, not just with spirits or souls. The entire believer, body and soul, is united with Christ.

This draws the Christian's body straight into Christian ethics. Because the body is a member of Christ, Paul argues, it must not be joined to a prostitute in fornication. The issue of "membership" is really an issue of "fellowship." What are you part of? Whom are you with? What larger thing than yourself do you belong to? The actions of the body are expressions of membership, fellowship, and unity. Therefore, certain bodily actions are excluded, and others are mandated.

The Christian's body is a temple of the Holy Spirit: habitation

Paul continues: "Or do you not know that your body is a temple of the Holy Spirit who is in you, whom you have from God?" (I Corinthians 6:19) In this statement, Paul moves from the concept of membership to that of habitation, and from the person of Christ to the person of the Holy Spirit.

The church is *corporately* the temple of the Holy Spirit. In I Corinthians 3:16-17, addressing issues of heresy and church unity, Paul addresses the Corinthians as the temple of the Holy Spirit with the plural you: "You [all of you together] are the temple of God . . . for the temple of God is holy, and that is what you [all of you together] are."

If the whole church is God's temple, then the correlated truth is that *each individual believer* is a temple of the Holy Spirit as well, and that is the form of address in I Corinthians 6. "Do you not know that your [singular, individual] body is a temple of the Holy Spirit?" That the church is the corporate temple of the Holy Spirit precludes heresy and schism; that the individual believer is a temple of the Holy Spirit precludes sexual immorality.

What does it mean that the Holy Spirit dwells in the believer's body?

To explain this, we must step back for a moment and make an essential distinction between God's *omnipresence* and God's *presence*. That God is omnipresent means simply that he is always and everywhere present by virtue of his deity and infinity. He is infinitely outside the space he has created, and he fills the space he has created – which we call the universe – like the water in the ocean fills a small sponge that floats within it. God is not "in" the universe. The universe is "in" God. He transcends it, and permeates it. God in his omnipresence is just as present in the cold desolation of Pluto as he is in a church service; just as present in hell as in heaven; just as present in the body of an unbeliever as in the body of a believer. So God's omnipresence in not, in itself, a doctrine of much comfort or gospel. It is simply true.

But the Bible more often speaks of God's "presence" as the manifestation of his existence in grace and friendship. He is everywhere present but he is not everywhere revealed and seen. In the days of the patriarchs, God revealed himself in intermittent and temporary fashion; Jacob met God and named the place "bethel," house of God. With the making of the law covenant with Israel on Sinai, God established his presence in a more permanent and accessible form, namely, the tabernacle. When Solomon built the temple on Mount Zion, this place of God's presence became even more solid.

The presence of God in the tabernacle and the temple was the "shekinah glory," a fiery manifestation which was located in the inner core, the cubical room called the "most holy place." The Greek word for this most holy place, *naos*, is the word which Paul uses in I Corinthians 3 to denote the church as a temple, and in chapter 6 to denote the believer's body as the dwelling place of God's Spirit. When Paul says, therefore, that the believer's body is a temple, he is not saying simply that God is omnipresent, but that the Christian's body is the exact, new covenant counterpart of the most holy place in Moses' tabernacle and Solomon's temple! It is not a poetic metaphor, but a statement of fact.

Now we must take this idea another important step. In the tabernacle and the temple, the presence of God made everything else in proximity to it "holy." The stones and timbers and curtains and utensils of the temple, though made of ordinary materials, became holy through their proximity to the shekinah glory. This meant that once something was consecrated for use in the temple, once it was made holy, it could never again be used for any other purpose. The holy things of the new covenant are not inanimate objects, but living persons, the persons whom Christ has saved and in whom he has come to live by his Spirit. So believers are called "saints," or holy ones. We are wholly given over to God, for his purposes and use, because he has set his presence in our bodies. We are the spoons, the altars, the curtains, the stones, the priestly robes, the censors, and the arks of the new covenant.

The Christian's body is the property of God: ownership

The Christian's body is a member of Christ, and a temple of the Spirit. It is also the property of God. "For you are not your own, you have been bought with a price; therefore glorify God in your body" (I Corinthians 6:20).

It's a hard concept for a modern American, schooled in democracy and freedom, weaned on the doctrine of individual autonomy, to digest, this biblical concept of being owned. It sounds a lot like slavery, and we got rid of that! We are jealous of that freedom-protecting space around ourselves and our bodies. We are sensitized to any threat to personal liberty. If there is one thing over which the modern American is indisputably sovereign, it is his or her body. This philosophy expresses itself in innumerable ways, both small and large, and most diabolically in the pro-abortion claptrap about "a woman's right to her own body," which is used as a cover for the murder of the unborn child's body. The idea of being owned physically by another is, in our culture, remote to the point of unreality.

Yet the New Testament declares in plain language, and without embarrassment or hesitation, that God owns his redeemed people. When Paul proudly calls himself the "slave of Jesus Christ," as he does in Romans 1:1 and elsewhere, he uses the ordinary, garden variety Greek word "slave" (though some modern translations soften this to "servant"). The authority of God over the people who confess him is as absolute as that of the owner over the slave. Believers are "a people for [God's] own possession" (I Peter 2:9).

Slavery to God extends to the Christian's body. Paul, scanning the surface of his own body and seeing there the scars and welts from beatings, imprisonments, and stoning, declares with joy his slavery to Jesus Christ: "From now on let no one trouble me, for I bear in my body the brand marks of Jesus" (Galatians 6:17). Slaves in the first century were often branded for identification; Paul's scars are the ownership marks of Jesus. Being owned by God is not a pretty metaphor, but a literal and physical reality which means that my bodily conduct in this present age is God's vested interest.

"You are bought with a price," says Paul (Romans 8:3). What price? The price of Christ's own bodily life, given up on the cross, is the purchase price of the believer's body. God the Father exchanged the body of his only begotten Son for the bodies of his people. This is what establishes the value and the dignity of the believer's body. The chemist may explain that my body is a few dollars' worth of elements, and the platonist may remind me that my body is a weak, aging, deteriorating, death-bearing vessel, and they are both correct from their limited viewpoints. But God thinks otherwise. God gave the body of his Son to buy my body, and by that act of free, uncoerced grace he sets the value of my body forever.

The believer's body is elevated to a lofty spiritual dignity by virtue of its membership in Christ, its habitation by the Holy Spirit, and its possession by God. So the platonist may scoff at the suggestion that lowly, disintegrating flesh can bring about the glorification of God, but the Christian believes that in Christ, resurrection energy has already gone to work in his body, and that his body is a fit instrument for the service, worship, and glorification of God. The believer sees his body as God does.

But now we must confront the materialist. The platonist objected that the body is not worth using. The materialist objects that the body is too valuable to be used.

Should we use up the body in the service of Christ?

The problem with using something is that it wears out. The materialist, we recall, believes that he has only his body, and he is therefore under tremendous pressure to make the preservation of his body the great purpose of his life. Christians, living in a world of materialists, are affected by this worldly valuation of the body, even though we do not believe the doctrine that underlies it. Christians drive down the same commercial avenues as everyone else, and as we pass the health insurance companies, and the doctors' offices, and the fitness centers, we hear the same screaming message that the extension and maximization of bodily life is the great good. We may know in our theology that this is not true, but the repetition of the message is bound to affect us. On Sundays we may celebrate eternal life and tell stories of men and women who have given up earthly life for the sake of the kingdom, but on Mondays we return to the service of our bodies.

It is also possible for Christians to act like materialists through the back door, as follows: in light of the body's spiritual dignity – for which we have argued in the previous section – we can make the preservation and care of the body into a kind of spiritual crusade, avoiding germs, eating

108

scientifically, working out religiously, and steering clear of all danger, all under the slogan "my body is the temple of God." I knew a man, years ago, who had a fabulous 1966 cherry red and white Mustang. Every inch of it was perfect, right down to the stitching. It sat covered in his garage, driven only enough to keep the engine running and the fluids circulating. He didn't really use this car because he knew that if he took it out onto real roads, for real travel, that it would get dings and chips and road grime and that the sun would shine down on the white vinyl and deteriorate it. He decided that he would rather preserve his Mustang than go places in it.

Is this God's intention for the Christian's body? Clearly not, according to the New Testament. For the apostle does not say, "Glorify your body." He says, "Glorify God in your body." The preservation of the body is not an end in itself. God has redeemed the body, filled it with his Spirit, and joined it to Jesus Christ, not to make the body a museum piece, but to use it. Faced with the materialist's objection that the body is too valuable to be risked or used, Paul replies that the believer's body is a *vessel*, a *weapon*, and a *sacrifice*.

The body is a clay pot

The people of Paul's day carried and stored things in clay pots. Some were simple and utilitarian, and others were elaborate and stylish. They were ubiquitous. So Paul's original readers knew right away what he meant when he wrote: "But we have this treasure [the gospel] in clay pots, that the surpassing greatness of the power may be of God and not from ourselves; we are afflicted in every way, but not crushed; perplexed but not despairing; persecuted but not forsaken; struck down but not destroyed; always carrying about in the body the dying of Jesus, that the life of Jesus also may be manifested in our body" (II Corinthians 4:7-10).

Clay pots, as everyone knew, wore out and broke. You could keep a clay pot forever if you never used it or filled it or carried it anywhere, if you put it on the shelf and admired it. But if you used it as a vessel, it would wear out.

The Christian's body is a clay pot. It is a vessel which God has created and purchased, not for his admiration but for his use. And God knows that the vessel will wear out in the using. Paul thought much about this, because he could see and feel what apostolic ministry was doing to his body. It was killing him. It was shortening his life. He had, according to the catalogue of II Corinthians 11:23-37, been imprisoned more than once (and imprisonment in that era was a health-breaking experience), repeatedly beaten by Jews and Gentiles, stoned, shipwrecked and adrift at sea; he had gone hungry and thirsty, he had been cold, and he had gone long nights without sleep. All this, be it remembered, Paul had endured without the help of modern medicine or the advantage of modern nutrition. Luke the physician was a smart man and a faithful friend, but there was little that even he could do to stave off the destruction of Paul's body. Paul was spending his bodily life for Jesus, carrying about the precious cargo of the gospel in his body, and in the process the clay pot was chipping and cracking and would one day break apart.

The believer's body, like a clay pot, is meant to be used.

The body is a weapon

The believer's body is also a weapon. We encounter this concept in Romans 6, where Paul is expounding the nature of the lethal struggle between the old lord, sin, and the new Lord, Jesus Christ, for the ethical territory of the believer's life. The old sin-dominated person has been executed with Christ on the cross ("our old man was crucified with him," v.6); the authority of sin has been broken ("that we should no longer be slaves to sin," v.6); a new life has started ("consider yourselves to be dead to sin, but alive to God," v.11).

This transformation occurs in the believer's core, the heart, but the struggle spreads immediately to the realm of the body's life. The Christian has been crucified with Christ "that our body of sin might be done away with," by which Paul means the body as it was under the lordship of sin and of the perverted appetites. And the new life that flows from the cross is a new bodily life: "Therefore do not let sin reign in your mortal body that you should obey its lusts" (v.12).

The Christian's body is the battleground where the old lord, sin, and the new Lord Christ struggle for mastery. There are no platonic victories. Sin aims to conscript the body for deeds of selfishness and wickedness, and Christ claims the body for righteousness. And it gets right down to the body parts. "Do not go on presenting the members of your body to sin as weapons of unrighteousness; but present yourselves to God as those alive from the dead, and your members as weapons of righteousness to God" (v.13). It is nothing less than a battle for the eyes, ears, mouth, hands, feet, and sex organs of the believer.

The word *hoplos*, which I have translated "weapon"

111

in the passage above, has a broad range of meaning. It can mean instrument, or tool, or weapon. A *hoplos* could be a plow, or an axe, or a hammer, or a sword. Romans 6 is about violent warfare and Paul certainly has "weapon" in view when he calls the believer's body parts *hopla*. In any case, whether weapon or tool or instrument, when you use it, it takes a beating. The finest sword is dulled and nicked in battle. If you use it for its intended purpose, it will wear. You will sharpen it for each new conflict, but it will lose a bit of metal each time and eventually it will wear out. The same is true of saws, and hammers, and plows, and surgical tools.

So the believer does not glorify God in the body by protecting his body like a museum piece from the wear and tear of living a holy life and serving God in a sinful world, but by sending it into the thick of the conflict. The struggle against sin will be harsh. The enemies will fight back against the believer's body, which is their only accessible point of attack. The body will suffer and wear, and finally, at some time and in some manner appointed by God, the weapon which is the believer's body will be used up and die.

The body is a sacrifice

The apostle Paul's most extraordinary language about the expendability of the body comes in Romans 12:1: "I urge you therefore, brethren, by the mercies of God, to present your bodies a living and holy sacrifice, acceptable to God, which is your spiritual service of worship."

The image of the clay pot took us to the marketplace, and the image of the weapon took us to the battlefield; now Paul takes us to the altar. Beside the altar is the priest, ready to do his primary work of offering sacrifice. But we are not looking at an Old Testament Levite priest, or at a sheep or ox as the sacrifice. In the image of Romans 12:1, the priest is every believer and the sacrifice is his or her own body. This is a startling thought. I must offer up my own body to God as a sacrifice. What does this mean?

Not, certainly, that the believer is to literally kill himself. The Christian's body is a *living* sacrifice, not a dead one. And the service envisioned is a "spiritual service of worship." The word translated "spiritual" here is a technical term which the Greek philosophers used to denote religion based on thought and reason as opposed to blind, traditional ritual. Paul plunders the word in this passage to emphasize the spirituality of Christian worship in the body. We must understand, therefore, that the sacrifice prescribed by Paul takes place, not on a literal altar but in the ethical life of the believer. The priests of Baal and Asherah cut, stabbed, and mutilated their bodies in their efforts to reach their gods, and the prophet Elijah laughed at them.

But if Paul is not envisioning a physical bloodletting, he is envisioning something just as drastic and violent in the ethical realm. After all, he could have said, "Give your bodies to God," or "Commit your bodily life to God," in language not taken from the gory and deadly work of the old covenant priests. But with the term "sacrifice" he brings to mind a work of bloody execution, of men with blood-spattered arms and robes, of squalling animals and dead corpses. This is because the consecration that God requires of the believer in his bodily life is as absolute as death, and because the believer will have to put to death his lusts and priorities, and because doing this will feel sometimes to the believer like he is cutting himself apart. The New Testament holds no punches here. Paul knew what it felt like. And Jesus knew what it felt like, because he became a man and took a body. He knows what it will feel like for a Christian young man to deny himself sexual pleasure until marriage. He knows what it will feel like to exercise moderation amidst the mountains of food and the gluttonous eating of the wealthy. He knows what it will feel like for the martyr to confess the gospel even when he can see the gallows, or the axe, before him. All this will feel like self inflicted death. So he tells it straight out, through Paul: *Christian, your obedience to me in the body is sometimes going to go against your deepest instinct for pleasure, life, and comfort. So get ready. Christian, your job is not to preserve and perpetuate your body, but to offer it up to me. You are a priest, and your sacrifice is your own body, and your job is to offer it up to me over and over again, so that I can use it for my purposes and my glory as I see fit.*

Divine life in dying bodies

Having steered our course between the falsehoods of platonism and materialism, we have ended in the middle of a remarkable paradox. The Christian's present, pre-resurrection body is made wonderful by its connection to Jesus Christ and its habitation by the Spirit and its possession by God, and it is to be used – and ultimately used up – in the service of Christ as a vessel, weapon, and sacrifice. This is the place of the body in the Christian life.

The apostle Paul identifies the paradox in his own way in II Corinthians 4:11: "For we who live are constantly being delivered over to death for Jesus' sake [the body is being expended], that the life of Jesus also may be manifested in our mortal flesh [the body bears and reveals

114

Christ's power and glory]." It is God's good pleasure to purchase and fill the believer's body, and to consecrate it for holy use, and then to use it.

If we understand this about our bodies, we are protected both from an overvaluation of the body, which leads to idolatry, and from an undervaluation of the body, which leads to a detachment of Christian holiness from the creation and from real life. Now we must return to our consideration of the body's appetites and see what happens to them under the sanctifying influence of grace.

CHAPTER 9

How to Glorify God in the Body

As we begin this last chapter of our study, let us see again where we stand.

We have learned that the human body is truly human; it is man. We have learned that it is fallen, that it is subject to the power of death, and that its desires and needs are perverted by sin. But there is redemption for the body in Jesus Christ, who assumed a mortal body and then a risen body in order to establish for us the hope of an identical resurrection. We have learned that even our present, mortal bodies are fitted for the glorification and service of God by their relationship to the Father (ownership), the Son (membership), and the Spirit (habitation).

We stand ready for action, in the body. While we wait for the resurrection, there is something important to do: glorify God in our bodies. We have learned why we must do this, and how it is possible to do this. Now we must suggest concrete action.

I say "suggest" because the practical outworking of divine glorification in bodily life is as comprehensive and unique as each individual believer's life. There is a sense in which each believer must write his or her own version of this final chapter, taking account of location, age, occupation, marital status, health, and calling. Each disciple is accountable to his Master. But we can draw some broad strokes.

The body is involved in almost everything

Our interest in this chapter is those issues having directly to do with the Christian's body. It should be remembered, however, before we come to those issues, that the body is involved in a broad range of ethical actions which are not specifically physical. This is the case because the body is the vehicle through which we come into contact with the world and with other people. If we consider, for example, something as central to holy living as the way we speak, we have Jesus' statement, "Out of the abundance of the heart the mouth speaks" (Matthew 12:34). Now speaking is not really a body issue; it is a heart issue. But even here the body is the instrument. If we consider, as another example, an act of mercy like giving a cup of cold water to thirsty person, we are looking again at something which reveals the love and compassion of the believer's heart. But the action of love must be performed with the hand. There is no way to speak, or to give the cup of water of the piece or bread, without using the instrumentality of the body.

The actions of the body are a revelation of the heart. My body is the servant of the purposes of my mind. In the broadest application, the glorification of God in the body must include everything that the believer does in and through the body.

But there are some issues which have directly and intrinsically to do with the body and its life and appetites.

Taking reasonable care of the body

The believer has a holy obligation to take reasonable care of his or her body. While there is no biblical text which states this in so many words, it is an inescapable implication of the themes we have already studied.

If the believer's body is the temple of the Spirit and a member of Christ and God's property, then it follows that the believer may not willfully neglect or destroy the body. If my body is a member of Christ, then any action against it is an action against Christ; if my body is a temple of the Spirit, then its neglect or destruction is vandalism. The sober warning of I Corinthians 3:16-17, "Do you not know that you are a temple of God, and that the Spirit of God dwells in you? If any man destroys the temple of God, God will destroy him, for the temple of God is holy, and that is what you are," though directed at destruction of the corporate temple of the church through heresy and schism, certainly also applies to the individual temple of the believer's body. And if my body is God's property, then I am not its owner but its steward, and I cannot simply do what I want to it.

The same mandate arises from another direction. We have learned that it is God's will to use the believer's body for his purposes in the world. It is God's instrument and weapon. Soldiers sharpen and polish their swords,

118

workmen clean their tools, and surgeons purify their instruments. A healthy and vigorous body is more useful to God than a weak, sick, tired and neglected body. When Paul instructs Timothy to "use a little wine for the sake of your stomach and your frequent ailments" (I Timothy 5:23), his main motive is certainly to help Timothy be a more effective minister of the word. Indigestion, ulcers, or nausea do not enhance the work of Bible study and teaching. When Jesus withdrew periodically from the huge crowds that followed him, it was, among other purposes, to recover physically from exhaustion and stress. Even Jesus would have been a dull instrument in God's hands if he had been physically incapacitated.

A third truth which implies the obligation of reasonable care is the integrity of the human person: the body and soul form one person, one organism. A human being is a "living creature." This means that the life of the body and the life of the inner person are intertwined; what is going on with the body affects the thinking, feeling, and deciding. So it is unbiblical and platonic to say, "I will neglect my body so I can give full attention to the cultivation of my heart." It won't work in the long run. A weakened body will bring the soul down just as surely as a weakened soul will vitiate the body; the two are one. Mental stress and fear and dejection can produce illness, heart disease, and insomnia; likewise, bodily pain and sickness can overwhelm the spirit. This being the case, the Christian who desires to cultivate the life of the Spirit in the inner person does well to take good care of the body too. Many a "spiritual" crisis can be best ministered to by a good night's sleep or a long walk.

But what is "reasonable"? We may begin with the obvious things. Christians may not kill themselves.

Christians may not wantonly destroy or mutilate their bodies. Christians should eat, and sleep, and practice available hygiene to sustain the health and strength of their bodies. But beyond these clear prescriptions it is difficult to go with any kind of authority, because of the lack of biblical authority, the complexity of bodily life, and the need for certain risks and sacrifices for the sake of Christ. Still, it may be helpful to point out two areas of bodily life where each believer must decide, before God, what reasonable care of the body means. These areas are exercise and the use of harmful substances.

Is exercise a holy obligation?

It is beyond dispute that exercise is good for both the body and the mind, but does that constitute a holy obligation? There is little explicit teaching in the Bible to help us here. Paul makes a cryptic comment about physical exercise in I Timothy 4:8, but it is not clear whether it should be translated "Exercise is of little benefit" or "Exercise is of a little benefit," that is, whether Paul is denigrating the value of exercise or simply emphasizing the relatively greater value of godliness. In either case, the verse falls short of being a biblical mandate for exercise. But if the doctor says, "Joe, if you don't start getting some exercise, this stress is going to kill you," it seems to me that Joe is now under some obligation to God to take better care of his body. If Betty's constant exhaustion, which hinders her church attendance and her performance at her job, could be ameliorated by some exercise, then it seems to me that she must exercise. We must stop short, however, of seeming to impose exercise as an obligation for believers in any comprehensive or absolute way. Although we don't know for sure, it is unlikely that the Lord Jesus Christ worked out. He was too busy spending his body for the sake of the kingdom. Each believer must stand before God with a clear conscience, and each believer must use wisdom and common sense. The issue here is not health, or tight muscles, or even feeling good for the sake of feeling good. The issue is the sharpness of the sword.

Substances old and new

What about the use of chemicals, substances, which harm the body? We include in this question alcohol, drugs, medications, and food products. Does reasonable care of the body involve the absolute renunciation of anything that adversely affects the believer's body?

For obvious reasons, the Bible does not address all of our modern substances, but it does address alcohol, and we can use the biblical approach to alcohol as a model. In the Bible, drunkenness is clearly identified as a sin and is forbidden (Ephesians 5:18). But the moderate use of alcohol is just as clearly not forbidden. Paul counsels Timothy to use wine for the sake of his digestion (I Timothy 5:23); the Lord tells the Israelites who were too far from the temple to bring their tithe to buy "wine and strong drink [beer]" with it and celebrate at home (Deuteronomy 14:26). Psalm 104:15 extols, among God's good gifts, "wine that gladdens the heart of man." Jesus drank wine, and Jesus created wine, and the wine which Jesus created was not nonalcoholic grape juice, as the whole story of the wedding at Cana shows (John 2). In light of such biblical evidence, it is an extra-biblical legalism to impose total abstinence on Christians' consciences. By extension, it is also out of line to impose a ban on things such as caffeine, cholesterol, preservatives, or foods grown with herbicides or pesticides, even though it is scientifically clear that there is probably some adverse effect on the body. It is just as certainly clear that ingesting caffeine or any other substance to the point where it is incapacitating the body or the mind is sinful, just as drunkenness is sinful.

As far the use of illegal drugs is concerned, the very fact of their illegality makes their use a sin. Christians are to abide by the laws of Caesar when those laws don't directly contradict the laws of Christ. Beyond this, the use of chemical substances in order to get "high" – that is, to alter consciousness – is sinful for the same reason that drunkenness is sinful: it is God's will for believers to be self controlled (I Peter 5:8 and many other verses). Alcohol, marijuana, heroin, cocaine, hallucinogens, and such drugs drastically alter a person's reason, perception, and inhibitions and intrude into the holy territory that the Spirit occupies in a believer's will. Getting high is a perversion of creation; it changes the created function of the mind just as homosexuality changes the created function of sexuality.

But even here, it seems to me there is a small space where the use of substances to alter consciousness is not sin. I refer to the legitimate medical uses of drugs to alleviate pain. A strong general anesthetic certainly alters consciousness – it makes you unconscious! – but it is not sinful if its purpose is to alleviate the pain of surgery. A man who drinks alcohol to intoxication before having his arm sawed off is not guilty of the sin of drunkenness, nor are those who are heavily dependent on morphine or (in Europe) heroin for the relief of chronic pain morally guilty

122

of substance abuse. There are medications for depression and other psychological conditions which may be used by the Christian with moral freedom.

The principles of moderation, self control, and compassion have much to do with how we steer between hedonistic substance abuse on the one hand and a pharisaical legalism on the other. And there is one more principle, often forgotten: consistency. It seems sometimes like Christians have their favorite "evil" substances. For some, it is alcohol, for others, tobacco, for still others, refined sugar. Jesus' teaching about judging others by the same standard you are willing to be judged by is relevant here. Many who passionately condemn even the most moderate use of alcohol eat to excess and are damaging their bodies far worse than those who drink a glass of wine from time to time. Many who stand in judgment on smokers are themselves addicted to caffeine. What is probably best is for us to stay out of the territory of other believers' consciences, except in the most blatant cases of drunkenness or use of illegal drugs, and tend to our own behavior. Each believer is accountable to God, and each believer must work out, under Christ's lordship, what reasonable care of his or her body means. We should not be surprised if the exact form of this obedience varies somewhat from disciple to disciple.

In all the decisions that relate to the care of the body, we must be aware of the danger that reasonable care of the body for the sake of Christ can easily slide over into "preservationism," which is an obsession with health and physical well being for its own sake. Christ is the Lord of the Christian's body. Christ may spend the body or use it for his purposes, and in that spending our bodies may be worn or even destroyed. The purpose of reasonable care is not to keep our bodies *from* Christ's use or from the wear and tear that serving Christ may entail, but to keep our bodies *for* Christ's use.

Disciplining the appetites

It is the calling of every believer, not only to care for his or her body, but to subordinate it to the purpose of God's glory. This brings us back to the appetites. The body, as we have seen, has its own compelling agenda: food, sleep, pleasure, sex, and survival. If we were not fallen, we would instinctively and gladly subordinate this bodily agenda to the will of God. But the body, along with the whole person, has fallen into bondage to sin and the appetites have been drafted into the service of unrighteousness. When Jesus redeems us, he sets us free from the bondage of sin, and we are now free, as we were not before, to submit our bodies and their members to his service. And we should. But because of our "history," and because we carry into the Christian life the habits and propensities of our bodily appetites as they were perverted by sin, the submission of our bodies is not instinctive and natural. Our legacy weighs down upon us. Perverted lusts are always lying in wait, needing only a breath of permission to spring into action. Therefore, we must learn to say no to our bodies; we must learn to deny them what they want.

The world system, dominated by materialism, coaxes us toward the idolatry of bodily life. The propaganda of the world system tells us that it is sick and dysfunctional to say no to one's body. The body, after all – the world says – is "natural," and what is natural is good. But the Bible says that what is "natural" in a fallen world is not good. So we must resist the propaganda and learn to say no.

The Bible alludes to several disciplines of the body, measures which the Christian intentionally undertakes for the purpose of subduing and training the appetites. The body cannot be subordinated to Christ's will if the appetites have their way all the time. The disciplines are a way of getting the body used to hearing that "no" and obeying.

The disciplines are like athletic training. When a high jumper wants to develop strength in his take-off leg, he does not merely do high jumps. He does deep squats, and plyometrics, and endurance exercises. The sprinter whose specialty is the 100 meter dash runs 200s, and 300s, and distance. The purpose of training is to tax the body beyond the limits of the event, so that in the event the body will be in a comfort zone. Likewise, the disciplines which we consider here are not to be practiced for their own sakes, but for the sake of bringing the appetites of the body under control in ordinary life decisions.

Saying no to food

We begin with fasting. Fasting is a disciplining of the body's appetite for food. It's purpose is not physical; it is not a "diet."

Fasting has copious biblical warrant; in spite of this, it is seldom practiced in modern evangelical piety. There is no appetite so untrammeled in our churches as the body's lust for food. Gluttony is scarcely considered a sin. To suggest that it is a sin is to invite chuckles. I know this from experience.

Perhaps what we need is some fasting. The New Testament does not command fasting, much less set down any patterns or rules for its practice; rather, the New Testament just assumes that the followers of Jesus will fast. Jesus fasted, and Jesus assumed that his disciples would fast (Matthew 6:16-18, "*When* you fast . . ."). The Christians of Acts fasted at crucial times (Acts 13:2-3, 14:23). Paul fasted (Acts 9:9). If the people of the first century, living as many of them did on the margins of adequate nutrition, needed to fast, then how much more do we, in the midst of our mountains of food and rivers of drink, need to bring this appetite under control?

Why fast? Fasting in the Bible often happens in tandem with prayer (see Daniel 9:3). Prayer requires the concentration of the soul's energies on God, who is invisible; to pray we must by faith leap across the sensory and material boundaries that define reality for us in our everyday lives. The day will come when we will not need to "pray" as we do now, for we will see the face of Christ and we will commune with him as we do now with one another, face to face, body to body. But for now, we must believe, and pray. And fasting is a companion to prayer.

The Christian elders and teachers in Antioch prayed as they commissioned Paul and Barnabas as missionaries to the Gentiles. Along with this praying, they fasted (Acts 13:2-3). Why? Because their agenda was to discover the will of God, but the agenda of the body was for them – and always is – to eat. As we pray, what happens at lunch time? Does the body get its way every single time? The body gets its way with food often enough, doesn't it? Aren't there some times with God that are too important, too precious, too painfully achieved, and all too rare, to be broken into for the sake of sandwiches and chips? When we have really come into contact with the invisible God, do we stop to eat? The elders and teachers in Antioch thought no. They said no to their bodies and yes to prayer.

It might be objected that a hungry body will be more of a hindrance to prayer than a fed body. This has a certain logic to it, but it is simply not what happens. The appetites, like spoiled children, feed and flourish on indulgence; when denied and subordinated, they grow quiet.

Christians should pray, and when prayer is of unusual importance or intensity, Christians should fast. Jesus assumed that we would.

Saying no to sleep

The body's demand for sleep is every bit as insistent as its demand for food, and there is some sketchy evidence in the Bible that times of "watching" – staying awake even when tired, saying no to the sleep appetite – are appropriate for Christians. The psalmist speaks of nights spent in prayer, and of rising to pray in the middle of the night (Psalm 6:6; 42:8; 63:6). Jesus spent all night in prayer (Luke 6:12). Paul mentions "watchings," or sleepless nights (II Corinthians 6:5), although it is not clear in this passage whether this is a voluntary discipline or something thrust upon him by circumstances.

The primary purpose of watching, as of fasting, is to clear the way for prayer. It is not fitting that the body's demand for sleep should always be heeded, especially when the believer needs to pray. The student denies himself sleep for the sake of the final exam; the taxpayer stays up late to get his taxes completed for the April 15 deadline; the traveler rises early to catch her flight. Why can't, why shouldn't the Christian say no to the sleep appetite on those occasions when prayer is important? When the body's agenda conflicts with the Spirit's agenda, the believer must say no to the body.

Saying no to sex

The sexual appetite is different from eating and sleeping in that its satisfaction is not necessary for the physical survival of the person – for the race, yes, but for the individual person, no. The body can live without sex. There are several biblical expressions of sexual denial.

First, and most obvious, is the sexual denial that each believer must practice before marriage. In modern western culture there is a mine-strewn time gap between the onset of the sexual appetite at puberty and the time when that appetite may be legitimately satisfied, at marriage. During this time, the adolescent Christian must say no to sex. And, beyond adolescence, all Christian adults who are not married must say no to sex. But the believer intent on purity will get no help at all from the culture, from the schools, or from peers. The culture regards sex the same way it regards eating and sleeping, as a natural appetite that must be given its outlet. Sex education in the public schools – and I have observed this personally – is dispensed on the assumption that teens will have sex, and its object is to help them have sex without getting a disease or getting pregnant. This is a terrific crucible for a Christian teen. Growing up in America, he has probably never had to deny himself anything, nor has anything this important ever been entirely up to him. It is the first fiery test of his loyalty to Jesus Christ. Jesus wants him, or her, to say no to sex until marriage.

Then, in marriage, Jesus wants the believer to continue saying no to sex – to all sex, that is, with any other person than the marriage partner, the husband or the wife. This, too, is a significant limitation of "natural" animal freedom, aptly expressed by the bumper sticker "So many men, so little time." But Christians make solemn covenants with their mates, and in those covenants they promise to say no to everyone else, and they promise to say no to their bodies.

The Bible is also clear that Christ calls some specially chosen believers to celibacy, that is, to lives without sex. When Jesus speaks of those who have "made themselves eunuchs for the sake of the kingdom of heaven" (Matthew 19:12), he is speaking euphemistically of voluntary celibacy, and of himself. The disciples have concluded, from Jesus' words on divorce, that "if the relationship of the man with his wife is like this [i.e. divorce forbidden except in the case of adultery], then it is better not to marry." To this idea that it is better not to marry, Jesus replies, "Not all men can accept this statement, but only those to whom it has been given." In other words, celibacy is a special gift from God, a special gift and calling to say no to sex permanently and completely and to be blessed in that denial. And the purpose of such a gift? Paul (who had received the gift himself) speaks to this: "But I want you to be free from concern. One who is unmarried is concerned about the things of the Lord, how he may please the Lord; but one who is married is concerned about the things of the world, how he may please his wife, and his interests are divided" (I Corinthians 7:32-34). Freedom from sex is freedom from marriage, and freedom from marriage is freedom from a whole worldly agenda that often competes with the

129

believer's ability to serve the Lord. So, when examined, the radical denial of the body's sexual appetite involved in celibacy is no different from that of fasting or watching. It is a way of centering the life on God.

One other form of sexual denial mentioned in the Bible conforms almost exactly to the pattern of fasting. Paul writes to Christian married couples: "Stop depriving one another [i.e. don't deprive your spouse of sex] except by agreement for a time, that you may devote yourselves to prayer..." (I Corinthians 7:5). There is an appropriate time, even in marriage, to say no to sex. It must be by mutual agreement – which prevents its use as a weapon in marital conflict – and it must be temporary, for Paul adds, "... and come together again lest Satan tempt you because of your lack of self control." Its purpose, as we might expect, is prayer.

Sex is a voracious appetite, and the Lord has ordained vigorous measures to bring it into submission: absolute, comprehensive denial before and outside of marriage; rigorous limitation to one person within marriage; lifelong denial for those with a special celibate calling from God; and temporary denial within marriage for the purpose of prayer. Very few differences between the disciples of Jesus and those who live for their own lusts will be more stark than this willingness to say no to sex.

Saying no to pleasure and toys

The body, as we saw earlier, craves pleasure as a thing in itself, quite apart from survival or procreation. The body craves relief from pain, pleasurable sensations, recreation, and pleasure-giving chemicals like alcohol and

130

drugs. The satisfaction of this appetite can transform the body into an idol.

The ability to satisfy this pleasure appetite usually depends on the possession of, or easy access to, things. The pursuit of pleasure, that is, takes money. Medical care takes money, and the finest medical care takes lots of money. Swimming pools take money, and RVs, dirt bikes, and boats take money. Drugs and alcohol take money, as do air conditioning and central heating, and reclining chairs.

I am suggesting that if we talk about the discipline of the pleasure appetite we will find ourselves talking about money and possessions. It is true that money is also the vehicle of another hunger, not of the body but of the sinful human heart: power. Some people, it seems to me few, pursue wealth as the path to power. These are those interesting individuals who have wealth but still live like ascetics. But most people who pursue wealth do so because of the pleasures it brings. They plan to buy things with their money – bigger and more comfortable houses, more expensive leisure activities, and more enjoyable retirements.

As I wrote the first draft of this book, Californians passed through a lottery frenzy. The "take" rose to $120 million. I will admit that the thought passed through my mind, "What would I do with $120 million?" The first, instinctive answer was, "I wouldn't have to work any more!" When I really think about this response, it seems that it arises, in large measure, from my body's appetite for pleasure. When $120 million looms up in my imagination, my body says, "Hey, let me rest, give me a break, pamper me! I've been serving you now all these years. Do something nice for me!" My daily work lands me exhausted in bed every night. This is what people who buy lottery tickets are thinking: no more work!

The body's pleasure appetite, then, is much more comprehensive than may appear at first glance. It operate powerfully even in the decisions of people who do not have decadent "lifestyles." How is it to be disciplined?

Biblically, the discipline of the pleasure appetite begins with the voluntary renunciation of things, and of money. Jesus commanded a young nobleman, who was otherwise a serious and pious person, to sell all his considerable possessions before he could follow Jesus. The young man said that he was willing to keep all the commandments, but Jesus perceived that the pleasure appetite was this young man's idol, and that it was being fed by the young man's wealth, and so Jesus simply said, "Sell all that you have." If you want the fire to go out, you have to stop putting wood on it. This the young man was not willing to do (Matthew 19:16-22). At this Jesus turned to his followers and said, "It is easier for a camel to go through the eye of a needle than for a rich man to enter the kingdom of heaven" (Matthew 19:24).

Those who followed Jesus had to renounce things, and money. "Behold, we have left everything and followed you; what then will there be for us?" (Matthew 19:27) It is impossible to devote one's life to the pleasure of Jesus and the pleasure of the body at the same time. Paul says, "If we have food and covering, with these we shall be content" (I Timothy 6:8). And he goes on to warn that "those who want to get rich fall into temptation and a snare and many foolish and harmful desires which plunge men into ruin and destruction, for the love of money is a root of all sorts of evil, and some by longing for it have wandered away from the faith, and pierced themselves with many a pang" (I Timothy

6:9-10). It's almost like Paul was peering across the centuries and looking at middle class America, and the millions in Los Angeles on the freeways, on their way to work to get money and on their way out of town to spend it.

The situation is clear: a life centered on the pursuit of money, things, and pleasure – that is, hedonism – is incompatible with a life centered on Jesus Christ. Since, as Paul reminds us, nothing that we possess in this world can be taken out of it at death or the judgment day (I Timothy 6:7), there can be only one motivation for the accumulation of things beyond what is needful to sustain life, and that is pleasure.

Is hedonism, like gluttony, one of the sins we take less seriously these days? Does the church view a person who spends conspicuously on himself the same way it views a fornicator, or a drug user, or a drunkard? Why not? If Paul could be content with food and covering, why can't we?

What do we do? "Instruct those who are rich in this present world not to be conceited or to fix their hope on the uncertainty of riches, but on God, who richly supplies us with all things to enjoy. Instruct them to do good, to be rich in good works, to be generous and ready to share . . ." (I Timothy 6:17-18). God certainly does give to some Christians the ability to earn more money than they need to provide food, drink, shelter, and clothing. It is not the earning of this money that constitutes hedonism, but the frivolous spending of it on self. When God bestows wealth on one of Jesus' followers, it is because he has chosen to use that person as a conduit for blessing to others. Wealth is given to be given. A Christian may be wealthy but may not live wealthy. Giving will require voluntary renunciation,

133

and voluntary renunciation will not be a mere abstract concept, but will be no Jacuzzi, no motor home, no lavish vacation, no early retirement. It will require the Christian to say no to his body's appetite for comfort and pleasure.

Saying no to life itself

The strongest appetite of the body is the appetite for life itself, the survival instinct. In order to glorify God in the body, the Christian must be prepared to say no even to this.

We are talking, of course, about martyrdom. While martyrdom is a remote eventuality for modern American Christians, it is a present reality in the teaching of the New Testament and in many parts of the world today. "Do not fear those who kill the body, but are unable to kill the soul" (Matthew 10:28). Among the "cloud of witnesses" whose faith we are to imitate are those who "were tortured, not accepting their release, in order that they might obtain a better resurrection . . . They were stoned, they were sawn in two, they were tempted, they were put to death with the sword . . ." (Hebrews 11:35, 37) These are the martyrs of the old covenant. Among the illustrious martyrs of the new covenant are Stephen (Acts 7), James (Acts 12:2), and Antipas (Revelation 2:13). And the glorious roll call could be extended through church history, down to the present hour.

In terms of our present study, a martyr is simply a believer who says the final "no" to the body and its appetites. Martyrdom is not self designed or self inflicted. The 16th century Spanish mystic, Teresa of Avila, undertook a missionary journey to the Moors in order to achieve martyrdom. She came back alive and disappointed, but if she had been killed, it would have been more like suicide than like martyrdom. Someone today could attempt martyrdom by preaching in the streets of Riyadh or Teheran, but this is not God's will. Martyrs are not Christians who want to die – there's no particular glory in being put to death when you want to die! – but Christians who want to live, who through God's providence are faced with the ultimatum of denying Christ to save their lives, and who choose to die rather than to deny Christ.

Bodily life is not an ultimate loyalty. There are things worth dying for. If the people of this world can give up bodily life for their various causes, then certainly the followers of Jesus Christ can give up bodily life for him and for truth.

Restoring the bodily dimension to discipleship

Let's face this fact honestly: very seldom do we actually say no to our bodies for the sake of Christ. There have been times in the church's history when earnest Christians have taken the denial of the body to excess – when fasting, for example, has passed from discipline to destruction, or when celibacy has been mandatory rather than voluntary, or when martyrdom has become a self congratulatory display for its own sake – but our time, at least here in American culture, is not one of them. The hallmark of our time is not denial of the body but its deification and pampering.

We must learn how to repudiate in our daily living the materialism that sets the body up as lord. We must turn from this modern idol. Jesus is the Lord, and our bodies are his weapons and his property.

We must learn how to work out, before God and his

word, the proper balance between reasonable care of the body and denial of the body's insistent appetites.

Where does the power come from?

It won't be easy. We have made our bodily appetites all the more insatiable through long indulgence. Where will the power come from to say no?

First of all, the power will come from the Holy Spirit. "If by the Spirit you are putting to death the deeds of the body, you will live" (Romans 8:13). By his presence in the Christian's body, the Holy Spirit not only dignifies it, but he also disciplines it. When the Christian is tempted by platonism, the Spirit declares, "This is my temple!" When the Christian is drawn into materialism, the Spirit declares, "This body is the weapon of Christ!" The Spirit is the agent of God's sovereign, transforming power in every part of the believer's ethical life, including the life of the body.

The power of the Spirit is the power of the resurrected Christ. The power of the believer to submit the body to the glory of God comes, therefore, through the Spirit from the resurrection power of Jesus Christ. "Newness of life" is resurrection life (Romans 6:4). This resurrection life is already flowing from the throne of Christ in heaven into our still fallen and dying world through the thoughts, emotions, and bodily actions of believers.

Living already in the resurrection

This is one of the great marvels of grace, that the life of eternity, the life that will begin in its fullness after the ringing of the final trumpet has faded away and the smoke has cleared from the fiery purging of judgment, begins even now. It would be glorious enough if God had promised to begin this life in our resurrection bodies, in which case we would simply wait in hope. But he has done more. He has ordained that the power of Christ's own resurrection, which has already taken place, be unleashed in us now, in this life, on this present earth, and in these present dying bodies.

It is as if the life to come is so full, so glorious, so unspeakably powerful, that its energy breaks the barriers of historical sequence and pulses backward from the judgment day into the present world, like a mighty reservoir so full that the abundance spills over in rivulets and streams, from which we can drink as we wait for the dam to fully burst. We drink of this future life in many ways. Our justification is the enjoyment of God's final verdict before the judgment day. The love and fellowship of the church is a foretaste of the fellowship of eternal life. The possession of the Spirit is a sampling of the intimate union with God that we will enjoy in the consummated kingdom.

And the submission of our bodies to the glory of God, and the using of our bodies as weapons of God, and the denial of our sinful appetites for the sake of God, are nothing less than an anticipation of resurrection life in a new heavens and earth.

Afterword

November, 2010
by Hannah Rainbow Ploegstra

My father's faith in the goodness of our physical bodies, their worth, and the affection of God towards them was a faith I witnessed through every facet of his life. He ate, worked, relaxed, exercised, and served others out of this faith. Even as a child, I knew from watching Dad that my own body was an instrument to be used for God's glory, not to pursue my own selfish ambitions or hungers.

What you have read in this small book is more than a collection of teachings or a compilation of the findings of a Bible scholar. This book gives words to a reality, a vision of the human body from Scripture, that my dad sought to live out faithfully each day. He'd cringe at my saying so--of course he was a sinner and, like us all, he struggled in the battle between the flesh and the spirit. But I can testify that he believed these things, because I learned them from him, not through a book like this, but by watching the way he lived.

The climax of this study, this book, cannot be read in its pages. It was written without words in the way he lived out the last 8 months of the life God gave him. In August of 2009 he was a vibrant, healthy, 4-mile-a-day 58-year-old man, and by the following June, 2010, he was dead. A terminal brain tumor, by God's sovereign, wise decree, took his life.

During his short illness, Dad sorrowed over the departure he knew he would soon experience--a departure from his children and grandchildren, from my mom, from this beautiful world of music and stories and prairie grass, and, not least, from his precious body of clay. He sorrowed in those days, yes, but he also rejoiced. The closer he got to death, the more single-mindedly he spoke of the resurrection--Christ's, and his--my dad's--own resurrection. He didn't want to talk about anything else. As he lost his grip on his own ability to care for and invest his body, he clung ever more fiercely to Christ's promise to do so on his behalf. Nothing mattered as much to my dad in his last weeks as this: that Christ would raise him again in a glorious new body, free from sin and free from death.

Now he is gone from us. His body lies in a North Dakota cemetery, waiting. We wait with him. Sometimes I envy him. In his spirit, the part of him that feels and understands and loves, he's there. He's there with the One who loves him, who took on flesh and died for him--the Living One. Along with all the believers who have already died--Abraham, David, Paul, Martin Luther, Jonathan Edwards, maybe some of your loved ones--my dad is there in his spirit, without sin, without pain, and without sadness.

But sometimes I think those souls which wait, the souls of those who have reached the finish line and understand now how worth-it the race was, as they're cheering us on, could it be possible that, in a sinless way, they also envy us? For we are still in our bodies--sinful, yes, but still precious and *useful*. Without a body, a man cannot sing, or hug, or dance for joy, or build, or shout. Only when the trumpet sounds will they be made whole. The creation groans. Bodies of clay, buried under the dust, groan for redemption and for resurrection. I think, in the midst of all his joy, my dad still groans to be made whole again. I still think, if he could, he'd be shouting about the resurrection.

God has given me a new relationship with my dad now. It's a strange kind of relationship, one in which we don't talk together, we don't sit together, we don't see each other or hug each other. Nevertheless, it's a real, living relationship, centered on Christ--a relationship of waiting together.

Waiting is a powerful form of fellowship. Waiting together, groaning together, keeps you focused on the thing for which you are waiting. Waiting alone, you can forget what you're waiting for. But waiting together helps you remember. Together with all the saints in heaven, we are all waiting, hoping, trusting, groaning for our bodies to be freed from the tyranny of death. Sometimes we forget that this is what we are waiting for, but it is. We are creatures, created to live out the image of God in these bodies of flesh, and as such we will not be completely, eternally happy, until that flesh is made new. The resurrection is what we all need. It's what we all want. It's what we're all waiting for. Our spirits want bones, muscles, tendons, voices, that can serve perfectly for all eternity, the Living God. Only when we have these will the Creator of our bodies, the Author and Perfecter of our faith, rest from *all* the work of creating that he has done.

Made in the USA
Charleston, SC
04 December 2010